Biblical & Social Justice: What Is it?

An Everyday Person's Guide to Understanding Justice
And the Role of the Church in Our Society

Bryan Hudson, D. Min.

visionBooks & Media
Indianapolis, Indiana

Biblical & Social Justice: What Is it?

An Everyday Person's Guide to Understanding Justice
And the Role of the Church in Our Society

ISBN 978-1-931425-04-9

©2020 Bryan Hudson

PUBLISHED BY
visionBooks & Media
Indianapolis, Indiana
www.visionbooksmedia.com

Printed in the United States of America

TABLE OF CONTENTS

Acknowledgements

I thank God through Christ for His grace to empower inspiration, research, and writing in this season of life. All of the life experiences, undergraduate and graduate learning, pastoral ministry, community service, and interactions with people from across the United States, the United Kingdom, Nigeria, and Kenya have informed my worldview. Thanks to my wife and best friend, Patricia, for her support and editing skills.

Special thanks to the following friends and scholars who have assisted, advised, and provided invaluable support:

Stephen E. Gardner, Ed.D.

Jimmy L. Hayes, Th.D.

Kenneth E. Sullivan, Ph.D.

Malcolm D. Magee, Ph.D

John Mastrogiovanni, D. Min.

Ophelia Wellington, M.A.

Jerry M. Williams, JD., Ph.D

FOREWORD

There have been a multitude of books written on the subject of Justice in order to inform the reader, but few, if any, have been published to transform the reader. Dr. Bryan Hudson's book—*Biblical and Social Justice, What Is It?*—has immeasurable transformative value, as a guide for the "everyday person" and any reader to understand Biblical justice and the role of the Church in our society. The author challenges the Church and its followers to actively engage the fight while living out the principles of Biblical justice and the righteousness of social justice. The book presents relevant insights, perspectives, and "food for thought" and real motivation for positive change in society.

Biblical and Social Justice, What Is It? gives us the opportunity to right wrongs of the past; to repent and rebuild towards a better future for us and our children. **I highly recommend this book** to those who are ready to embrace the truth, change, and strive for progress!

~ **Jerry Miah Williams,** J.D., Ph.D.

It is a rare occasion when a book comes along that feeds both your mind and soul. This book does exactly that. With scholarly skill, and plain spoken language, Bryan Hudson speaks to the current situation in our country. This book draws its strength, however, not merely from current experience, but from an accurately focused understanding of our history. The commentary on Dr. King's, Letter From a Birmingham Jail, is worth the price of the book, and it is but one gem in this storehouse. Reading this will compel not only attention but action as well.

~ **Malcolm D. Magee,** Ph.D.
Professor
University of Maryland Global Campus, Europe

The Christian Church has stood on the sidelines confounded and divided at times when it comes to understanding its role and the proper application of justice. On the one hand, Evangelical believers lack consensus about its perception and practice. On the other hand, Roman Catholics, are more unified in their perspective on social justice, through the teachings of Thomas Aquinas' system of ethics, which is fundamental to modern Catholic social teaching. However, in the book *"Biblical & Social Justice: What Is It?"* Dr. Hudson delivers exactly what the subtitle states, *"An Everyday Person's Guide to Understanding Justice and Role of the Church in Society."*

This book is written in the style where the person sitting in the pew or the person leading their congregation from the sacred desk can easily understand the meaning, the challenges, and the application of justice. Dr. Hudson explores both historical and contemporary matters that pertain to justice in the church and justice in society. Regardless of your Christian denomination, you will leave from reading these pages inspired, and possessed with a renewed sense of commitment to the church's call to justice.

~ Stephen E. Gardner, Ed. D.

Bryan Hudson has given us a compelling resource exploring the distinction between Biblical and social justice and how they connect and function. Confusion about what Biblical justice is and whether it should, or should not, intentionally affect social justice is an issue that is still being hotly debated in Christian circles and has resulted in a kind of paralysis among some Christian segments. Hudson makes the persuasive argument that social justice is the outworking of true Biblical justice and that true Christianity, lived the way Jesus advocated, does not exist in a vacuum. This book is timely, relevant, and carries the conversation about justice forward, especially during this season when the attention of the world is drawn to this important subject.

~ Kenneth E. Sullivan Sr. Ph.D.

INTRODUCTION

He has shown you, O man, what is good; And what does the Lord require of you but to do justly, to love mercy, and to walk humbly with your God? (Micah 6:8)

Justice is both a reality and a dream. It is a source of hope and of frustration. Justice, like a mountain, affords many perspectives depending upon which side one is viewing.

For persons who are well-established in life, justice is a wall of protection. For persons struggling with obstacles or battling mistreatment, justice is a door through a wall. The appropriate interaction between Biblical justice and civil justice is difficult to define. On one end, is full separation between church and state. On the other end, is extremist dominion theology or Christian nationalism that proposes full integration of the Christian church into the affairs of the state.

Within a democratic republic such as the United States of America, there is a two centuries old tension between viewpoints and applications of justice. On balance, the nation has been well served by our Bill of Rights and Constitution. Freedom of religion has flourished under a philosophy of government that has not made the Bible our law. Christianity, the predominant faith in the nation, has not suppressed other religions such as Judaism, Islam, or variants of the orthodox historic Christian faith such as the Church of Latter Day Saints and Seventh Day Adventists.

As a nation founded in rebellion to the King of England, George III, and the state Church of England, the Constitution has proved itself as a successful model of governance and foundation for civil justice — notwithstanding notable failures and gross injustices such as American slavery as well as the mistreatment of Native Americans in forced migration from their lands.

11

What is not as clear is the success of the church as it relates to doing Biblical justice. The terms "Biblical justice" and "civil justice" will be highlighted throughout this book as separate, but complimentary concepts. There is also the term "social justice" which is controversial due to narratives, some intentionally false, that social justice is a rejection of the Word of God and an embrace of some form of Marxism. This is little more than guilt by association. This tactic is not unlike denigrating every form of the statement, "Black Lives Matter" when most of us are not talking about the organization, but the human reality, "Black lives matter." For the purposes of this book, social justice will represent the practical application of Biblical justice in society.

> The conditions of today have been determined by what has taken place in the past. (Carter G. Woodson)

The goals of this book are to shine a bright light of insight and to educate readers by increasing understanding of both scriptural mandates regarding justice and unbiased lessons from history. It is also the aim of this book to bring matters related to racial minorities out of the historical shadows.

About the Writing Style of this Book

The title of this book is *Biblical & Social Justice: What Is It? An Everyday Person's Guide to Understanding Justice and the Role of the Church in Our Society.* The term "everyday person" is not intended to offend the status or intellect of any person. The intent is to present material in a manner that is easy to read and understand. The writing style is informal and conversational. Many resources have been read and researched. These are available in the bibliography of this book.

There are two books I want to highly recommend as foundational to understanding justice and the role of the church. The role of the church in society has not been entirely positive and unfortunately has too often been highly detrimental to the cause of Christ and equal justice.

The first book: *White Too Long: The Legacy of White Supremacy in American Christianity* by Robert P. Jones[1].

This is the most substantial and well researched book I've ever read on the subject of race, white supremacy, and the documented role of the church in North America. By it's honest telling of history, Robert P. Jones provides an immense level of hope for our future progress. No telling of American history or presentation of a "Christian worldview," is complete without a resource such as this book.

The other book: *Woke Church: An Urgent Call for Christians in America to Confront Racism and Injustice* by Eric Mason[2]. As an African-American pastor and scholar, Dr. Mason brings a high level of practical understanding and insight into how today's church can effectively serve God's purposes and our communities.

In a world of opinions and low information, it is essential that we have a firm grasp of facts, both historical and contemporary. The best opinions and concepts are formed from deep understanding. There are portions of this book that are difficult to read. It is important to accept those portions, not as a stimulant for guilty feelings, but as food for thought and motivation for change.

This book will present many insights and opinions, which I will offer as one man's perspective. I trust you will find these insights relevant, reliable, valid, and useful to your life and our times. I welcome reader perspectives and challenges to recommendations and points of view presented in this book.

"The difficulty lies not so much in developing new ideas as in escaping from old ones." – John Maynard Keynes

~ **Bryan Hudson**, October 2020

---

1   Jones, Robert P., *White Too Long: The Legacy of White Supremacy in American Christianity*. Simon & Schuster. Kindle Edition.

2   Mason, Eric. *Woke Church*. Moody Publishers. Kindle Edition.

CHAPTER 1

~

What is Biblical Justice?

Learn to do good; Seek justice, Rebuke the oppressor; Defend the fatherless, Plead for the widow. (Isaiah 1:17)

There is no single, widely accepted definition of *Biblical Justice*. Research on Biblical justice reveals many definitions, theological expositions, articles, and books, that offer perspectives. It is a highly subjective term.

As part of research for this book, a survey was distributed seeking responses to a number of questions. One of those questions was, "What is Biblical Justice?" The survey responses may be reviewed in the Appendix.

Summary of Survey Responses

Survey responses show broad perspectives on the question, "What is Biblical justice?"

Respondent Six (R6) raised the issue of which part of the Bible should we consider for defining and applying Biblical justice, Old Testament or New Testament? R6 concluded, *"That which is modeled by the life of Jesus Christ."* Christians often speak and write about the importance of doing justice, but it is unclear what type of justice is being advocated. Respondent Two (R2) suggests Biblical justice is the *"application of God's law in society."*

Survey responses illustrate the disparate perspectives that exist regarding the application of Biblical justice.

To Whom Does Biblical Justice Apply?

Two problems to contemplate if one considers Biblical justice as something to be applied in society:

1. How do we persuade legislators (many of whom are non-Christians) to create laws using the Bible?

2. How do we compel unbelievers to believe and follow the Bible for the purposes of applying Biblical justice?

Respondents to the survey seemed to suggest two ways to consider Biblical justice. Firstly, there is the sense of justice as related to God's omnipresence and omnipotence. The Psalmist wrote, *"The Lord has established His throne in heaven, And His kingdom rules over all."* (Psalm 103:19) Secondly, there is the application of Scripture as specific codes and laws of Biblical justice.

What we see in the Bible is God establishing order for Israel around the law of Moses and the instructions provided in the Pentateuch (The first five books of the Bible).

Biblical justice is therefore covenant justice. It is the practical outworking of Israel's special relationship with God. Justice flows from a life of obedience to the law of God, a law that derives its character from a larger vision of shalom, of God's intentions for human life. Law, justice, and covenant are thus overlapping or interpenetrating concepts in the Bible.[3]

We also see God's Sovereign acts of Divine Justice (actions not defined in the book of the Law) as His judgment against Israel's enemies. It seems that Biblical justice, in the strictest sense of the term, were the instructions and acts of justice carried out among the people of Israel.

---

[3] Marshall, Chris. *Little Book of Biblical Justice: A Fresh Approach To The Bible's Teachings On Justice* (p. 15). Good Books. Kindle Edition.

At the time of Christ, the Roman Empire did not abide by Biblical justice (the Pentateuch) though they recognized that Israel had its own form of justice, as demonstrated when the Jews tried to persuade Pilate to punish Jesus, to which he responded, *"Then take him away and judge him by your own law," Pilate told them.* (John 18:31)

> Clearly, Biblical justice, as laws and the Scriptures, was not part of the Roman Empire which was idolatrous in nature. In Rome, government wasn't just absolute, it was literally divine. "Roma" was a goddess; all public offices were also religious offices; and executions for high crimes were sacrifices to the gods.[4]

Again, according to Psalm 103:19 God's kingdom (and Divine justice) rules over all in His Sovereignty.

The outworking of Biblical justice, or righteousness, was demonstrated by the actions of believers within the Early Church and through their witness to the life and power of Christ. They also engaged in works to assist one another as well as people in their communities.

> *In all things I have shown you that by working hard in this way we must help the weak and remember the words of the Lord Jesus, how he himself said, 'It is more blessed to give than to receive.* (Acts 20:35)

Therefore, it does not seem reasonable to make the case that Biblical justice should be applied to gentiles or non-Christians, though God remains the judge of all.

If the Scriptures were the law of the United States, that would be unconstitutional (the USA was not founded as a theocracy). Additionally, we would have a Christian version of "sharia law" as

---

4   Gobry, P. (2018, June 18). *What the Bible really says about government.* Retrieved September 10, 2020, from https://theweek.com/articles/779283/what-bible-really-says-about-government

practiced within Islamic nations— a form of government that would have been antithetical to the intentions of the Framers of the United States Constitution.

All things considered, I would agree with the following survey respondents:

R3: *"Biblical justice is to do what is right and just."*

R5 *"I believe Biblical Justice as defined in the New Testament and demonstrated in the life of Jesus is to provide equal mercy, grace, and resources to all alike regardless of position, racial background, or gender."*

Biblical justice is not expectations or codes **that we apply to others.** Biblical justice is what **we do** through the Spirit of Christ in obedience to God's word. Through this approach, we can positively impact the world around us as salt and light, up to and including, *"Learn to do good; Seek justice, Rebuke the oppressor; Defend the fatherless, Plead for the widow."* The justice systems of our nation, and other nations, remains intact and under the domain of citizens and lawmakers within democratic societies. Christ Followers remain in the world, but not of it. We exercise influence and Biblical justice.

> If *you were of the world, the world would love its own; but because you are not of the world, but I chose you out of the world, because of this the world hates you.* (John 15:19)

Biblical Justice - Social Justice - Justice

Looking at how the word *justice* is used in the Scriptures, I would suggest the following:

- **Biblical Justice** involves God's expectations for believers in Christ. Through His grace, He expects us to live a certain way among the community of believers and then to reflect His righteous Character to the larger society.

- **Social Justice** represents our engagement in society including, feeding the hungry, advocating for children, assisting the poor, or speaking out against injustice.

- **Justice**, when used alone, refers to civil justice, criminal justice, or jurisprudence, and the practice of laws and application of the justice system within our communities and nation.

Examples of the Word Justice in the Bible

There are 136 mentions of one form of the Hebrew/Greek word *justice* in the New King James Version (see the Appendix for specific definitions). There are 304 mentions of the other Hebrew/Greek word for *justice* which essentially means *righteousness*. Some key passages include:

Evil men do not understand justice, but those who seek the Lord understand all. (Proverbs 28:5)

He has shown you, O man, what is good; And what does the Lord require of you but to do justly, to love mercy, and to walk humbly with your God? (Micah 6:8)

Thus says the Lord: "Execute judgment and righteousness, and deliver the plundered out of the hand of the oppressor. Do no wrong and do no violence to the stranger, the fatherless, or the widow, nor shed innocent blood in this place." (Jeremiah 22:3)

Blessed are those who keep justice, And he who does righteousness at all times! (Psalm 106:3)

It is a joy for the just to do justice, But destruction will come to the workers of iniquity. (Proverbs 21:15)

What sorrow awaits you teachers of religious law and you Pharisees. Hypocrites! For you are careful to tithe even the tiniest income from your herb gardens, but you ignore the more important aspects of the law—justice, mercy, and faith.

You should tithe, yes, but do not neglect the more important things. (Matthew 23:23 NLT)

Summary of Insights and our Role in Society

All of these definitions suggest one primary conclusion: **Justice is related to righteousness.** The contexts of the words *justice* and *judgment* suggest the following:

1. One cannot preach righteousness without doing justice.

2. Justice must be done in the spirit of righteousness.

3. Authenticity is essential for one's lifestyle. Live according to Christ and the word of God.

4. One must take action in helping those who are disadvantaged.

5. Resist oppressors by holding persons accountable who would take advantage of others.

6. Stand up for those who cannot stand up for themselves.

We have to consider what justice looks like as it relates to our practice as Christ Followers and as citizens within society and culture. We are certainly not called to behave as "Christian vigilantes" in taking matters of civil justice into our hands.

In light of Scriptural injunctions about justice, what should be our best practices? How do we apply our mandate of justice in practical terms? These are questions to address in the next chapters of this book.

Reflection Questions

1. Why is Biblical justice difficult to define?

2. What is Biblical justice?

3. What is social justice?

4. How does social justice relate to Biblical justice?

5. What is the relevance of justice to righteousness?

CHAPTER 2

~

Social Justice and Church Engagement

Vindicate the weak and fatherless; Do justice to the afflicted and destitute. Rescue the weak and needy; Deliver them out of the hand of the wicked. (Psalm 82:3-4)

Learn to do right; seek justice. Defend the oppressed. Take up the cause of the fatherless; plead the case of the widow. (Isaiah 1:17)

We have considered the term "Biblical justice." Now, we will consider the term "social justice."

The subject of social justice carries the heavy baggage of preconceived notions. Like the third rail of an electric powered train carries high voltage electricity, there are "third rail" words that may trigger irrational or emotional reactions. The words "social justice" are among those highly charged words.

The following definition of social justice was suggested by Dr. Stephen E. Gardner;

Social Justice has both political and religious definitions in society. The perceptions of social justice among American Evangelical Clergy have the possibility to yield a variety of interpretations depending on the experiences of each clergy person.However, for the purpose of clarity, social justice is defined as efforts to relieve poverty and hunger, to promote world peace and justice, or as addressing local issues (Todd & Allen, 2011). [5]

A practical definition, such as this, of social justice goes a long way towards fending off misinformation and false narratives. For Christ Followers, social justice is the actual practice of Biblical justice and righteousness.

We should not allow misunderstanding or misinterpretation about social justice by a few to damage engagement, understanding and interpretation for all. Worse, is to allow bad theology to go unchallenged. The following statement is an all-too-common simplistic response to social justice from a spurious Christian perspective:

> The gospel of Jesus Christ is the only true theology of social justice and hope for the poor[6].

The author went on to claim the following,

> "Suddenly the Holy Spirit spoke to me: 'The present social justice movement is preparing the poor of the earth to receive the Antichrist.'" [7]

To a reasonable person, Christian or non-Christian, this statement is patently erroneous and misleading. Social justice (however it is understood) and millions of poor people, are not subject to one person's imagination. This is an area where Christians can be unhelpful.

Misplaced Convictions

Christianity is a faith of convictions, some based on the Bible and others based on mere religious tradition. A conviction is "a strong persuasion or belief."

While conviction may reinforce one's doctrinal integrity of faith in Christ, a religious or personal conviction can be detrimental. In the

---

[5]   Gardner, S. E. (2016). *Leading the practice of social justice through Evangelical congregations: A multi-case study.* Dissertation Abstracts International Section A: Humanities and Social Sciences. ProQuest Information & Learning

[6]   Greaves, Stuart. *False Justice: Unveiling the Truth about Social Justice* (Kindle Location 244). Destiny Image. Kindle Edition.

[7]   Ibid.

Bible the word convict (or reprove in KJV) means "to reprehend or admonish." Conviction can come from either the Holy Spirit or from one's conscience. Examples from Scripture:

> And He [The Holy Spirit], *when He comes, will convict the world concerning sin and righteousness and judgment.* (John 16:8)
>
> *The faith which you have, have as your own conviction before God. Happy is he who does not condemn himself in what he approves.* (Romans 14:22)
>
> *For our gospel did not come to you in word only, but also in power and in the Holy Spirit and with full conviction; just as you know what kind of men we proved to be among you for your sake.* (1 Thessalonians 1:5)

Religious conviction does not well serve addressing problems within our society. A personal religious conviction cannot guide others. It is intended to guide oneself. God grants freewill to people. He does not permit one person to hold valid convictions about what others should do. As it relates to people, conviction is the work of the Holy Spirit (John 16:8). Too many Christians presume to know the conditions of people's hearts and minds. Too many presume to understand the circumstances of others, to the point of the absurd notion that "poor" persons are likely to be influenced by the Antichrist —— as if affluent persons cannot be similarly influenced.

Presumption is a sin: *Keep back Your servant also from presumptuous sins; Let them not have dominion over me. Then I shall be blameless, and I shall be innocent of great transgression.* (Psalm 19:13)

It is a sad historical fact that people have used the Bible to assert or maintain control of political and social systems. American slavery was the worst form of this practice. In more recent times, we have seen the Bible misused in support of political parties and politicians. In August of 2020, then Vice-President Mike Pence made a speech were he conflated the United States Flag with Jesus Christ using portions of Hebrews 12:1-3 and 2 Peter 3:14-18:

So let's run the race marked out for us. Let's fix our eyes on Old Glory and all she represents. Let's fix our eyes on this land of heroes and let their courage inspire. And let's fix our eyes on the author and perfecter of our faith and our freedom. And never forget that where the Spirit of the Lord is, there is freedom. That means freedom always wins.[8]

Mike Pence crossed a bright Biblical line in comparing devotion to our flag ("Old Glory") with our Lord and Savior. For many Christians this has become an all too common error. It highlights a problem as old as our nation, regarding America as the Kingdom of God to a greater or lesser extent. Patriotism has its place, but it should never be confused with devotion to God. American citizens, Christian and non-Christian, embrace the Pledge of Allegiance, but a Scripture infused veneration of anything or anyone other than the living God is idolatry.

Again, Christianity (as a religious practice) can be very unhelpful when personal religious conviction is allowed to replace reason, research, sociology, and empirical evidence. For example, when presented with complex problems, a person of religious conviction might conclude: *"They just need Jesus."* The truth is, there are people in need who already know Jesus as Lord and Savior.

Every work of a Christ Follower does not have to be related to preaching or proselytizing. We can do charitable works or good deeds for the sole purpose of meeting human need. This is part of doing social justice through practicing righteousness in society. A Sovereign God knows how to draw people to Himself.

So then neither he who plants is anything, nor he who waters, but God who gives the increase. (1 Corinthians 3:7)

Below are Scriptures related to serving people socially with no proselytizing motive:

He who has pity on the poor lends to the Lord, And He will pay back what he has given. (Proverbs 19:17)

---

[8]   Full Transcript: *Mike Pence's R.N.C. Speech.* (2020). New York Times. https://www.nytimes.com/2020/08/26/us/politics/mike-pence-rnc-speech.html

I have shown you in every way, by laboring like this, that you must support the weak. And remember the words of the Lord Jesus, that He said, 'It is more blessed to give than to receive.' (Acts 20:35)

But love your enemies, do good, and lend, hoping for nothing in return; and your reward will be great, and you will be sons of the Most High. For He is kind to the unthankful and evil. (Luke 6:35)

Then the King will say to those on His right hand, 'Come, you blessed of My Father, inherit the kingdom prepared for you from the foundation of the world: 35 for I was hungry and you gave Me food; I was thirsty and you gave Me drink; I was a stranger and you took Me in; 36 I was naked and you clothed Me; I was sick and you visited Me; I was in prison and you came to Me.' (Matthew 25:34-36)

And the second, like it, is this: 'You shall love your neighbor as yourself.' There is no other commandment greater than these." (Mark 12:31)

And seek the peace of the city where I have caused you to be carried away captive, and pray to the Lord for it; for in its peace you will have peace. (Jeremiah 29:7)

And let our people also learn to maintain good works, to meet urgent needs, that they may not be unfruitful. (Titus 3:14)

Therefore, as we have opportunity, let us do good to all, especially to those who are of the household of faith. (Galatians 6:10)

The Case for Social Justice

God's church touches our world in many different ways. Some may view Christ's Church as a place to learn, to grow personally, become more Christlike, and to find purpose and happiness in life. This would reflect a more inward facing Biblical justice perspective.

Others may view Christ's Church as a place to reach out to the lost, to carry the gospel locally, behind prison walls, support missions, and relieve suffering. This would reflect a more outward facing social justice perspective.

The World Vision organization made a very significant statement about the term social justice:

> Don't be fooled or distracted by the word "social" in social justice. Many Christians are more comfortable with the word "justice," but if Christ is truly Lord over every aspect of our lives, then clearly this must also include the social realm...Biblical references to the word "justice" mean "to make right." Justice is, first and foremost, a relational term — people living in right relationship with God, one another, and the natural creation. From a scriptural point of view, justice means loving our neighbor as we love ourselves and is rooted in the character and nature of God. As God is just and loving, so we are called to do justice and live in love.[9]

Politically conservative evangelicals might hold to this definition of Biblical justice:

> We uphold Biblical justice when we render impartially and proportionally to everyone his due in accord with the righteous standard of God's moral law. (E. Calvin Beisner)[10]

I disagree with this statement. This writer seems to be framing Biblical justice on the model of the United States justice system. Using this definition, the question is: Who gets to decide what is the "righteous standard of God's moral law?"

Statements like this have a ring of truth, but it is also highly subjective and puts final authority in the hands of people who cannot represent the entire church or society.

Dr. Malcolm Magee, from his article, *The Dark Side of Religion in America*, wrote:

> If the church is to be truly universal, then it needs to remain both welcoming to all sides of the political debate and, potentially confrontational to all sides. The church must also acknowledge the right of other religions, and non-believers, to live in harmony in a

---

9   *What does social justice really mean?* (2020). World Vision. https://www.worldvision.org/blog/social-justice-really-mean

10 *What Is the Biblical Concept of Justice?* (2020). Word Foundations. https://www.wordfoundations.com/what-is-the-biblical-concept-of-justice-2/

harmonious civil society. If it does not, it will become loathsome to all. Just another institution of accrued power.[11]

Example of Social Justice by Believers in Christ

The church, for good or for ill, has been on the forefront of social change. As a force for social justice, Christ Followers have taken Biblical justice everywhere they go. Collectively and individually, we were told by Christ to be "salt and light," to take influence and illumination into every setting, from the marketplace to the workplace. An example of social justice at work outside the institutional church, yet influenced by Christ Followers is the non-profit, **The Children's Policy and Law Initiative of Indiana**. CPLI was established in 2013 to reform laws, policies and practices that contribute to the criminalization of children in Indiana. It is one of 53 organizations in 43 states that belongs to the National Juvenile Justice Network (NJJN). The NJJN leads a movement of state-based advocacy groups working toward a fairer youth justice system.

Mission Statement: CPLI advocates for systemic changes for children so that programs, policies and practices are developmentally appropriate, equitably administered and fair, and provide the necessary support for a child's successful transition to adulthood.[12]

Participants of CPLI come from a cross section of citizens, many of whom are Christ Followers, whose presence represents the best practice of faith in the workplace and marketplace. One of the members of our church serves in a leadership capacity with CPLI. The Children's Policy and Law Initiative of Indiana does good work in the area of social justice. They have formed committees working on behalf of children and families in areas such as:

Public Policy - The Public Policy Committee advocates for public policy changes that impact children at the state and local level.

---

11 Magee, Malcolm (2019). *The Dark Side of Religion in America.* Medium. https://medium.com/malcolmmagee/the-dark-side-of-religion-in-america-194b5e2fce9f

12 About CPLI. (2020). *The Children's Policy and Law Initiative of Indiana.* http://www.cpliofindiana.org/cpli-home.html

PSDI Planning - The Positive School Discipline Institute (PSDI) Planning Committee is coordinating a year-long initiative to train school personnel on positive school discipline strategies.

De-Criminalization - The De-Criminalization of Youth Committee focuses on reforming public policies that increase the risk of justice-system involvement.

Programs - The Programs Committee coordinates the planning of CPLI's annual public policy summit, supports a signature fundraising event, and plans other educational forums.

The Children's Policy and Law Initiative of Indiana is one example of a great number of similar organizations across our nation. From the perspective of this author, it is a positive example of social justice at work. Learn more about CPLI at *www.cpliofindiana.org*.

Christ Followers in the Marketplace

While the Biblical mission of the church is primarily preaching the Gospel, discipling believers, and serving human needs within our communities, members of the church are engaged at every level of society. This is consistent with guidance from the Scriptures,

Most assuredly, I say to you, he who believes in Me, the works that I do he will do also; and greater works than these he will do, because I go to My Father. (John 14:12)

For it is God who works in you both to will and to do for His good pleasure. (Philippians 2:13)

It is a mistake to make the assumption that the church is destined to take over institutions in society, that is reserved for a "New Heavens and a New Earth" under God. *Then He who sat on the throne said, "Behold, I make all things new." And He said to me, 'Write, for these words are true and faithful.'* (Revelation 21:5)

Our best practice today is to serve God's purpose in support of good works that may not be under the direct control of a local church. We have our ministries. We should respect the work of organizations in society and seek to participate as individuals when we are able to do so.

As stated earlier, Christian conviction does not always lead to good outcomes, especially when exercised outside of personal matters.

We have seen bad outcomes of Christian religious conviction in areas such as participation in partisan politics, endorsing candidates, and aligning with people of poor character and behavior. There has been the erroneous conviction that God has "chosen" political candidates. In reality, what we have witnessed is a Christian church that has failed to win hearts and minds by their service and witness to the world. Instead of focusing on the work of the Gospel and Biblical justice, power alliances have been formed with politicians to leverage, and sometimes co-opt, their secular offices to do the bidding of politically motivated Christians.

Those who use the things of the world should not become attached to them. For this world as we know it will soon pass away. (1 Corinthians 7:31)

Reflection Questions

1. Why is social justice not considered to be Biblical?

2. What is the Bible case for helping people within our communities and beyond?

3. How is Christian conviction helpful and unhelpful?

4. How can non-profit organizations do social justice along side of, and distinct from, the church?

5. What Scriptural and social justice action can we employ to help in the above issue?

CHAPTER 3

~

Social Justice and Preparedness to Act

My brethren, do not hold the faith of our Lord Jesus Christ, the Lord of glory, with partiality. For if there should come into your assembly a man with gold rings, in fine apparel, and there should also come in a poor man in filthy clothes, and you pay attention to the one wearing the fine clothes and say to him, "You sit here in a good place," and say to the poor man, "You stand there," or, "Sit here at my footstool," have you not shown partiality among yourselves, and become judges with evil thoughts? (James 2:1-4)

As stated earlier in this book, "social justice" is understood as the outworking of Biblical justice. Biblical justice applies to God's people through the teachings of scripture and the presence of the Holy Spirit. This is not available to people who are not in Christ. God is Sovereign and He reigns overall, but He is working through his church. Social justice is acting in society as a reflection of, and in obedience to, Christ. As Paul said in 2 Corinthians;

Now then, we are ambassadors for Christ, as though God were pleading through us: we implore you on Christ's behalf, be reconciled to God. (2 Corinthians 5:20)

Ambassadors do not impose their system of justice on the country they're serving. They allow the values of their country to positively impact people in the country they're serving. What Christians and churches do in society is a reflection of Biblical justice. Congregations located in needy parts of the city, tend to be more active because they are compelled to interact with people and their issues. They cannot only preach Jesus, they have to show His love.

In the opening text, James offered a scenario where two men came among a congregation. One man wore fine apparel, while the other man appeared to be poor and broken. This was an opportunity to practice the principles of Biblical justice, by not showing a preference, but by ministering to both men. Fine clothes that people wear may not indicate the state of their hearts. James stated it would be unjust to send the needy man away without something needful for his body.

So then, Biblical justice is not limited to the concepts we believe or the words we speak. It must contain the component of social justice, where we take positive action. God may send people or circumstances among us to test the sincerity and practicality of our faith. This is the mandate of Biblical justice, not what we impose upon others, but the righteousness we provide to others.

A socially active and relevant church will promote a correct understanding of God as being involved with the affairs of people. People will understand by our example that God is not trapped behind the walls of church buildings. He is actively working in every place and within every condition to bring hope and tangible action. All of this is empowered by the grace of God in Christ.

The Christ Follower's Unique Stand Amidst "Principalities and Powers"

Put on the whole armor of God, that you may be able to stand against the wiles of the devil. For we do not wrestle against flesh and blood, but against principalities, against powers, against the rulers of the darkness of this age, against spiritual hosts of wickedness in the heavenly places. Therefore take up the whole armor of God, that you may be able to withstand in the evil day, and having done all, to stand. (Ephesians 6:11-13)

Our engagement within communities and the larger society involves a number of factors from interpersonal, to governmental, law enforcement, political, socioeconomic factors, and much more. Undergirding and overarching those factors are spiritual realities which are known to Christ Followers.

Because we are grounded in God's word and in the nature of Christ, grace has provided a well formed perspective on life in relation to things visible and invisible. Christ Followers also learn to prepare to serve while trusting God to do the "heavy lifting." The Apostle James wrote, *"Thus also faith by itself, if it does not have works, is dead."* (James 2:17) Works do not create faith, but serve to verify the genuineness of what we believe God is doing. As we work, principalities, powers, and spiritual hosts are present in one form or another, including influences introduced by various types of people. The Apostle Paul did not go into detail in explaining the exact nature of these forces because it was not necessary to do so.

When believers in Christ follow Him and are obedient to the word of God that we know, the Holy Spirit handles unseen forces that we don't see. For example, when we pray and ask God for something, we don't need to try to figure out how God is going to do it. We only need to focus on having confidence in God to do what He does, while we pay attention to those matters that fall within our responsibility. Using an everyday example, when we press the start button in our automobiles and the engine starts, we don't think about all that's happening inside the engine to cause it to run. We only focus on regular maintenance and going where we need to go.

There's a story in 2 Kings Chapter 6 of the prophet Elisha and his servant being surrounded by an enemy. The servant became fearful about their situation. Elisha said to him, *"There are more with us than with them."* This statement did not ease the fears of the servant because all he could see was the enemy surrounding a place where they were. Elijah prayed a simple prayer for God to open the eyes of his servant. When he did, his servant saw the enemy surrounded by a host of angelic beings. It is not clear if Elisha initially saw the angelic host, but **he knew** they were there.

It is not necessary for us to see or understand everything God is doing, we only need to know that He's doing it. God always surrounds those who surround us.

When we faithfully handle matters that God has put in our charge, He will handle matters that are beyond our scope. This is the reason why Paul advised us to put on the *"whole armor of God"* that speaks to our best practices of spiritual preparedness. This preparedness is essential for our effective engagement in social justice.

> *No one has seen God at any time. If we love one another, God abides in us, and His love has been perfected in us.* (1 John 4:12)

Insights from Rev. Dr. Martin Luther King and the Church in His Day

In a 1965 interview that Alex Haley conducted with Rev. Dr. Martin Luther King, he offered compelling theological, prophetic and practical insights on the church's role regarding social action. Dr. King and the civil rights movement promoted social justice as the outworking of Biblical justice long before it was appreciated by the church. This is an excerpt from that interview.[13]

HALEY: Can you recall any other mistakes you've made in leading the movement?

KING: Well, the most pervasive mistake I have made was in believing that because our cause was just, we could be sure that the white ministers of the South, once their Christian consciences were challenged, would rise to our aid. I felt that white ministers would take our cause to the white power structures. I ended up, of course, chastened and disillusioned. As our movement unfolded, and direct appeals were made to white ministers, most folded their hands —and some even took stands against us.

HALEY: Their stated reason for refusing to help was that it was not the proper role of the church to "intervene in secular affairs." Do you disagree with this view?

Author note: *Today's evangelical church has moved away from this position and into full embrace of partisan politics. There is the merging of Biblical justice with civil justice, to the detriment of both.*

---

[13] Haley, Alex *Haley Interviews Martin Luther King, Jr.* (1965). Alex Haley. https://alexhaley.com/2020/07/26/alex-haley-interviews-martin-luther-king-jr/

KING: Most emphatically! The essence of the Epistles of Paul is that Christians should rejoice at being deemed worthy to suffer for what they believe. The projection of a social gospel, in my opinion, is the true witness of a Christian life. This is the meaning of the true ekklisia—the inner, spiritual church. The church once changed society. It was then a thermostat of society. But today I feel that too much of the church is merely a thermometer, which measures rather than molds popular opinion.

HALEY: Are you speaking of the church in general—or the white church in particular?

KING: The white church, I'm sorry to say. Its leadership has greatly disappointed me. Let me hasten to add that there are some outstanding exceptions. As one whose Christian roots go back through three generations of ministers—my father, grandfather and great grandfather—I will remain true to the church as long as I live. But the laxity of the white church collectively has caused me to weep tears of love. There cannot be deep disappointment without deep love. Time and again in my travels, as I have seen the outward beauty of white churches, I have had to ask myself, "What kind of people worship there? Who is their God? Is their God the God of Abraham, Isaac and Jacob, and is their Savior the Savior who hung on the cross at Golgotha? Where were their voices when a black race took upon itself the cross of protest against man's injustice to man? Where were their voices when defiance and hatred were called for by white men who sat in these very churches?"

As the Negro struggles against grave injustice, most white churchmen offer pious irrelevancies and sanctimonious trivialities. As you say, they claim that the gospel of Christ should have no concern with social issues. Yet white church goers, who insist that they are Christians, practice segregation as rigidly in the house of God as they do in movie houses. Too much of the white church is timid and ineffectual, and some of it is shrill in its defense of bigotry and prejudice. In most communities, the spirit of status quo is endorsed by the churches.

My personal disillusionment with the church began when I was thrust into the leadership of the bus protest in Montgomery. I was confident that the white ministers, priests and rabbis of the South would prove strong allies in our just cause. But some became open adversaries, some cautiously shrank from the issue, and others hid behind silence. My optimism about help from the white church was shattered; and on too many occasions since, my hopes for the white church have been dashed.

Martin Luther King's observations and frustrations in 1965 express similar challenges and frustrations in 2020. Dr. King said, "Some cautiously shrank from the issue, and others hid behind silence." This continues to be a challenge in our day when cultural pressure, or preference, leads to a lack of engagement from some ministers.

On the other hand, it is very encouraging to see strong engagement from others. I am acquainted with several White ministers, friends and citizens who are fully "woke" and strong advocates of both Biblical justice and social justice action. Preparedness to act has been present in every generation from the era of a young John Lewis leading Freedom Riders to scholars like Robert P. Jones (whose book is a key source for content in this book), justice has always been the work of citizens from diverse backgrounds.[14]

Photo Credit: Mississippi Department of Archives and History

---

[14] Taylor, D. B. (2020). *Who Were the Freedom Riders?* https://www.ytimes.com/#publisher. https://www.nytimes.com/2020/07/18/us/politics/freedom-riders-john-lewis-work.html

Reflection Questions

1. As Ambassadors for Christ, how do we fulfill Christ's work without imposing our Biblical mandate?

2. What is understanding all the unseen forces not necessary?

3. What was Dr. King's concern about working with some of the White pastors of his day?

4. What are three lessons you can take away from Dr. King's interview?

CHAPTER 4

~

The Reign of Narratives

With many things in life and society, what we believe often comes from what we have heard. Our understanding of justice is shaped by learning based on the depth of our hearing. Within the context of Jesus teaching His disciples about modes of receptivity in the Parable of the Sower, Jesus highlighted the importance of hearing in the Gospel of Mark,

> *Then He said to them, "Take heed what you hear. With the same measure you use, it will be measured to you; and to you who hear, more will be given. For whoever has, to him more will be given; but whoever does not have, even what he has will be taken away from him." (Mark 4:24-25)*

According to Jesus, what and how one hears are major factors to what one receives as well as the effect of those things on the hearer. The "measure" one uses to hear is measured, or applied, back to the hearer in the same proportion. In this Parable of the Sower, Jesus described four conditions of soil to the receptivity of seed. Those conditions represented four modes of one's heart. Three of the conditions did not allow the seed to flourish. The fourth condition described as "Good Ground" allowed the seed to flourish abundantly as described in Matthew's version of the parable,

But he who received seed on the good ground is he who hears the word and understands it, who indeed bears fruit and produces: some a hundredfold, some sixty, some thirty (Matthew 13:23).

The keys to fruitfulness were attached to, 1) Hearing, 2) Understanding, and 3) Becoming a Fruit Bearing Condition. "Hearing" accurately and intensely were factors to fruitfulness. Along with God's Word, the condition of one's heart and the preparation of one's mind for hearing are vitally important.

It is fascinating to hear descriptions of cities, people, groups, and nations. Many simply parrot what they have heard, as if their mind was preconditioned to seek neither accuracy nor understanding.

For example, I've often heard the phrase that Chicago is the "Murder Capital of the nation." When an acquaintance on Facebook made that assertion in one of his posts, I investigated and learned that Chicago was most certainly not the murder Capitol of the United States. Data from multiple years has not shown Chicago to have the highest rate of murder, per capita.[15] When presented with these facts, my acquaintance challenged both the data and myself from what appeared to be a "right wing" political perspective. He sent a link from a propagandist blog "proving" that Chicago was the "murder capitol." Reviewing the link, it became clear that I was dealing with a person caught up in a narrative, a false narrative in this case. His measure of "hearing" was faulty and it resulted in propagating a faulty measure of spreading an untruth.

We Have Become Dependent Upon Narratives

A narrative is defined as:

1. Some kind of retelling of something that happened (a story). The narrative is not the story itself but rather the telling of the story

---

[15] *Chicago is far from the U.S. 'murder capital.'* (2018). Pew Research Center. https://www.pewresearch.org/fact-tank/2018/11/13/despite-recent-violence-chicago-far-from-u-s-murder-capital/

2. A report of connected events, real or imaginary, presented in a sequence of written and/or spoken words.

3. Consisting of or characterized by the telling of a story.[16]

These words stand out, *"The narrative **is not** the story itself, but rather **the telling** of the story."* Facts are bound to an actual story. Things that happened are a permanent part of a record. Narratives are not bound to the law of facts, any more than a two hour movie can faithfully dramatize a person's entire lifetime. A narrative is like Cliffs-Notes™ for non-inquiring minds, a search for information without depth, insight, or context. A narrative does not have to be inaccurate, but it will certainly be limited in depth, and context may be at risk. As a high school student, I used CliffsNotes™, not to gain an understanding, but to get a passing grade on an assignment. Gaining mastery was not the goal, mediocrity and shortcuts were acceptable standards for me at that time.

Our Internet based Information Age affords many advantages related to quick access to information. The days of needing to visit a library to spend hours researching and browsing to find books and periodicals pertinent to our information needs, has long passed. A 60 second Google search yields more results than hours of researching books and periodicals in a library, but what is the value of those results?
For modern methods of research, two words have become essential in this age of instant information: **Reliability** and **Validity**. Simplifying these terms from the domains of research and education, *reliability* is about the consistency of a measure, and *validity* is about the accuracy of a measure.

On the matter of Chicago being the murder Capital of our nation, in order to be a reliable statement, data would have to be presented from multiple studies over time. Those studies would need to be consistent in the measurement of the Chicago murder rate in order to be considered reliable. In reality, multiple studies over the years have not

---

16 *Narrative*. (2019). Wikimedia Foundation, Inc. https://en.wikipedia.org/wiki/Narrative

shown Chicago to have the highest murder rate per capita. That said, **there is no acceptable rate of murder in any city.**

Validity has to do with the actual research and its methods for gathering data. It is unlikely that a lone person writing a blog, having a negative perception about Chicago, would be able to offer results with the same validity as researchers who have no bias for or against Chicago. A blogger may have heard that Chicago is the murder capital from another blogger or a news channel. This phenomenon is called an "echo chamber" where inaccurate information is repeated among people with a similar confirmation bias (which is the tendency to interpret evidence as confirmation of one's existing beliefs or theories). In this scenario, reality is set aside in favor of a narrative that represents mutual feelings of disdain, not facts. There are many narratives that are accepted among circles of people as fact. In reality, there are probably more narratives than actual stories. We are all aware of blatant false narratives such as NASA moon landings being faked in a studio or the earth being flat.

After the end of the Civil War, in which the Confederacy was defeated and slavery was abolished, work soon began on what became known as the "Lost Cause"[17] which was a significant effort in building a false narrative about the Confederacy. Rather than accepting defeat and fully re-integrating with the United States, Confederates through the United Daughters of the Confederacy (UDC) launched efforts to maintain White supremacist values and re-invent their image, not as defeated rebels, but as heroic Christians standing firm on Biblical principles.

These efforts succeeded in erasing gains made by African Americans during Reconstruction, including Black people holding elected offices in the Deep South, including a Governor in Louisiana, P.B.S Pinchback elected in 1872. Federal troops remained in much of the South until 1877 when a deal was struck to change southern electoral

---

[17] Jones, Robert P.. *White Too Long: The Legacy of White Supremacy in American Christianity* (p. 57). Simon & Schuster. Kindle Edition.

votes to support Rutherford B. Hayes in exchange for the removal of troops.[18] After the withdrawal of the federal protection put in place by President Abraham Lincoln, Black Americans faced a backlash of terrorist violence such as lynchings.[19] What became known as Jim Crow laws and Black Codes intensified after the removal of federal protection.

The UDC worked to establish some 1,747 monuments in honor of defeated Confederate rebels such as Jefferson Davis, Robert E. Lee, including tourist attractions like the giant carving into the side of Stone Mountain, Georgia, outside of Atlanta.[20] Researcher Robert P. Jones writes,

> Even the placement of the monuments in prominent public places was done with the next generation in mind. After dedicating a monument to Confederate soldiers in 1899 on the county courthouse grounds in Franklin, Tennessee, UDC leaders celebrated its educational value; that children "might know by daily observation of this monument" the values for which their ancestors fought. This message, obviously, was meant for white children and conveyed quite a different message—the continued assertion of white supremacy—to the African American children and adults in the community.[21]

Through these efforts, false narratives became tools for instilling a sense of pride in the face of unrepentant racism, inculcating a supremacist mindset in the southern white citizenry, and in children being trained. Narratives about white racial superiority became justification for marginalizing African Americans through "Black Codes" and

18 Rutherford B. Hayes. (2020). *The White House*. https://www.whitehouse.gov/about-the-white-house/presidents/rutherford-b-hayes/

19 *Reconstruction*. (2020). History Channel https://www.history.com/topics/american-civil-war/reconstruction

20 *Jones, Robert P.. White Too Long: The Legacy of White Supremacy in American Christianity* (p. 119). Simon & Schuster. Kindle Edition.

21 Ibid.(p. 113).

"Jim Crow" laws during the early 20th Century[22]. Added to this repression were terrorist acts against Black people to incite fear and assert control under the same old Confederate values of racial superiority.

In defiance to a United States Constitution that states, "All Men Are Created Equal" and in contradiction to the Bible that affirms that all people are made in the "Image and likeness of God," white supremacists, aided by Biblical justification supplied by the Southern Baptist Convention and others, the ultimate false narrative was created:

Black people were inferior to White people, are immoral, dangerous, and they must be subjugated and controlled.

Southern white Christians, particularly Baptists, played a critical role in justifying a particularly southern way of life, including what they sometimes referred to as the "peculiar institution" of slavery. Central to this story, but not widely known, are the efforts of the Reverend Dr. Basil Manly Sr. Born into a wealthy North Carolina plantation family in 1798, Manly followed his mother into the burgeoning Baptist movement in the South over the protestations of his Catholic father. Leveraging his influence as the senior pastor of prominent churches in South Carolina and Alabama, Manly became a pivotal leader in both religious and political secessionist movements. He was the chief architect of the withdrawal of Baptists in the South from cooperative fellowship with their northern brethren over the issue of slavery that established the Southern Baptist Convention; and he was instrumental in building a southern alternative to ministerial educational institutions in the North, which he perceived to be increasingly under the influence of abolitionists. Manly was widely recognized as the leading theological apologist for slavery in his day.[23]

---

22 *The Black Codes and Jim Crow Laws.* (2020). National Geographic Society. https://www.nationalgeographic.org/encyclopedia/black-codes-and-jim-crow-laws/

23 Jones, Robert P.. *White Too Long: The Legacy of White Supremacy in American Christianity* (p. 34). Simon & Schuster. Kindle Edition.

False narratives have indeed reigned in revising history or re-stating history for the benefit of people who refuse to learn by reading and study. In the 21st Century of a cable news, low information, and sound bite addicted citizenry, narratives have replaced deeper understanding.

Reflection Questions

1. What is the value of being a good listener?

2. How have false narratives hindered understanding of Black history?

3. What was the significance of United Daughters of the Confederacy?

4. What are some examples of distorted Christian doctrine supporting white supremacy and injustice against Black people?

5. What Scriptural and social justice action can we employ to help in the above issue?

CHAPTER 5

~

A Nation Founded on Christian Principles?

"Between the Christianity of this land, and the Christianity of Christ, I recognize the widest possible difference." ~*Frederick Douglass*, 1845

Any exploration of justice must include a discussion about the founding of our nation. Stating that the United States was founded on the Bible and on Christian principles is a source of great pride for many Christians in America.

> America was established by God for the propagation of the gospel across the globe and to demonstrate God's grace through a government that promotes and defends liberty. Of course, America has many blemishes and flaws. Our nation is neither perfect nor blameless. One thing we can say for sure is that America has been the best model of freedom this world has seen. [24]

There is no evidence that America was established for the purpose of spreading the Gospel around the world. It is true that freedoms afforded to many Americans allowed missionaries to travel abroad to spread the Gospel. At the same time Black Americans in the 18th and 19th centuries were enslaved, not allowed to learn or read, and denied "unalienable rights." An honest view of history reveals the brilliance of the United States Constitution as a governing philosophy that has stood the test of time, but ungodly deeds should not be overlooked.

---

[24] *America the Prosperous.* (2018). https://www.afa.net/the-stand/faith/2019/11/america-the-prosperous

Sowing ungodliness at the founding of the nation, reaped horrors later, as we shall learn.

It is typical for Christian nationalists (those who promote the view that America was founded by Christians on Biblical principles) to promote a narrative that pushes the horrors of injustice down to the level of "blemishes and flaws," like a bad paint job on an otherwise great car. Some attribute all outcomes to the Sovereignty of God, whether the enslavement of Africans, rape, wars, or massacres. Of course, God is Sovereign, but it is not for people to explain, understand, or use that truth as justification for wrongdoing or injustice. One of the most important attributes of God is His mercy towards us.

Survey Responses

On the question: *"Was the United States founded on Christian principles?"*

R1: No. How can a nation be founded on Christian principles when they stole the land from Native Americans, and they used slavery of black people to build it? There is nothing Christian about that. That's hypocrisy!

R2: Not all the founders of the United States were Christians, but most of them were (roughly 2/3). It is my understanding that the Founders who wrote the U.S. Constitution, wrote it based on principles that stemmed from a Biblical worldview that recognized God as the Creator and man as the created thing. And, that all authority is in God and He gives man limited authority over other men through a legitimate civil government. So, it is likely that the U.S. was founded on Christian principles; notwithstanding that two-thirds of the founders were slaveholders.

R3: No. The laws of this country condoned slavery which is contradictory to Christian principles.

R4: Yes. Look to documents of the Founding Fathers. Including, but not limited to, the U.S. Constitution.

R5: To some degree on Christian principles, as they were the dominant ideas in the colonies at the time. Certainly not "Biblical" principles as the only founder with a theological background was John Witherspoon and his theology was deeply influenced by the Scottish Common Sense Enlightenment. Henry May wrote a very good book on this called *"The Enlightenment in America"* where he argues that the Enlightenment and Protestant Christianity fought a battle at the founding and eventually Protestant Christianity emerged ahead by around 1800, but that it had been profoundly changed by its struggle with the Enlightenment and no longer looked like the Protestantism that had preceded the Revolution.

R6: No! For the sake of this research report, here is a short quote from our first American treaty submitted to congress by the former Vice-President to George Washington and then second President, John Quincy Adams: "As the Government of the United States of America is not, in any sense, founded on the Christian religion..." (Treaty of Tripoli, Article 11, May 26, 1797).

The Framers and the first President, George Washington, were aware of God, and it was customary to invoke His name on special occasions. On October 3, 1789, one week after Congress approved the Bill of Rights, President George Washington made an official Thanksgiving Proclamation[25]:

Whereas it is the duty of all Nations to acknowledge the providence of Almighty God, to obey his will, to be grateful for his benefits, and humbly to implore his protection and favor—and whereas both Houses of Congress have by their joint Committee requested me "to recommend to the People of the United States a day of public thanksgiving and prayer to be observed by acknowledging with grateful hearts the many signal favors of Almighty God especially

---

[25] Washington, G. (1789). *Thanksgiving Proclamation*. National Archives and Records Administration. https://founders.archives.gov/documents/Washington/05-04-02-0091

by affording them an opportunity peaceably to establish a form of government for their safety and happiness."

Now therefore I do recommend and assign Thursday the 26th day of November next to be devoted by the People of these States to the service of that great and glorious Being, who is the beneficent Author of all the good that was, that is, or that will be—That we may then all unite in rendering unto him our sincere and humble thanks—for his kind care and protection of the People of this Country previous to their becoming a Nation—for the signal and manifold mercies, and the favorable interpositions of his Providence which we experienced in the course and conclusion of the late war—for the great degree of tranquillity, union, and plenty, which we have since enjoyed—for the peaceable and rational manner, in which we have been enabled to establish constitutions of government for our safety and happiness, and particularly the national One now lately instituted—for the civil and religious liberty with which we are blessed; and the means we have of acquiring and diffusing useful knowledge; and in general for all the great and various favors which he hath been pleased to confer upon us.

And also that we may then unite in most humbly offering our prayers and supplications to the great Lord and Ruler of Nations and beseech him to pardon our national and other transgressions—to enable us all, whether in public or private stations, to perform our several and relative duties properly and punctually—to render our national government a blessing to all the people, by constantly being a Government of wise, just, and constitutional laws, discreetly and faithfully executed and obeyed—to protect and guide all Sovereigns and Nations (especially such as have shewn kindness unto us) and to bless them with good government, peace, and concord—To promote the knowledge and practice of true religion and virtue, and the encrease of science among them and us— and generally to grant unto all Mankind such a degree of temporal prosperity as he alone knows to be best.

Given under my hand at the City of New-York the third day of October in the year of our Lord 1789.

These were wonderful sounding words from the first president. Statements such as this are presented as evidence that the United States was founded as a Christian nation. References to "this people," "to render our national government a blessing to all the people," "the civil and religious liberty with which we are blessed," and "our safety and happiness..." did not include all people. One might think his words "pardon our national and other transgression" may have indicated his regrets about owning slaves and supporting slavery. Mary V. Thompson, a Mount Vernon historian wrote,

> "There wasn't much evidence prior to the revolution that he ever considered slavery to be wrong He's leading a war where people are saying that people are born free, that freedom is a God-given right," Thompson said. "And he's not stupid. He can see the hypocrisy of owning slaves."[26]

Invoking the name of God was, and is, a common practice. "In God We Trust" was first inscribed on U.S. coins in 1864 under President Lincoln. In 1956 Congress made "In God We Trust" the national motto of the United States. As we are all aware, invoking God's name and submitting to His will are often unrelated actions. Christian nationalists have long promoted romanticized narratives about the Framers of the United States.

> Perhaps above all, those who forged our nation's documents and laws were God-fearing people, with a basic Christian outlook on life, morals, and government, which set the course for maintaining the freedoms we now take for granted.[27]

26 Brockell, G. (2019). Mary V. Thompson, *Mount Vernon Historian (Interview).* *Washington Post.* https://www.washingtonpost.com/history/2019/08/25/george-washington-owned-slaves-ordered-indians-killed-will-mural-that-history-be-hidden/

27 Morris, J. (2001). *In What Ways Has God Blessed America?* Institute for Creation Research. https://www.icr.org/article/what-ways-has-god-blessed-america

Whatever the religious beliefs of the Framers, they decided not to make the Bible the explicit basis of the Constitution. The Constitution contains no references to Jesus Christ or citations   from Scripture, something that any Christian document would provide. There is also evidence that many of the Framers were influenced by their practice of Freemasonry, which many believers in Christ do not find consistent or compatible with the Biblical doctrine of the Lordship of Jesus Christ.

America's Wealth and Slavery

There is also the view that the great wealth of the United States and our cutting-edge innovations in areas of agriculture, industrialization, and, later, technology are evidence of the blessing of God. A detail that's often excluded from discussions about the wealth of our nation is the magnitude of the contributions of African American slaves and free slave labor from 1619 through 1865.

> Why would a slave have so much value? A short answer is the value of a slave is the value of the expected output or services the slave can generate minus the costs of maintaining that person (i.e., food, clothing, shelter, etc.) over his or her lifetime. A quick list of the data that have to be considered in determining the value of a slave's expected revenue would include sex, age, location, how much he or she is likely to produce (a factor that included a slave's health and physical condition), and the price of the output in the market. For a female slave, an additional thing to consider would be the value of the children she might bear. (Williamson & Cain)[28]

Slavery in the United States was an institution that had a large impact on the economic, political and social fabric of the country. [29] A study conducted by Samuel H. Williamson and Louis P. Cain gives an idea of its economic magnitude in 2016 values. The calculation re-

---

[28] *Measuring Slavery in 2016 Dollars*, Samuel H. Williamson and Louis P. Cain, https://www.measuringworth.com/slavery.php

[29] Ibid

vealed the astounding estimate that the value of slaves and slave labor in 1860 amounted to $14 trillion in 2016 money. [30]

Listening to the stories of Christian nationalists, one might become persuaded that the United States descended from heaven.

Any assertion that the United States was founded on Biblical and Christian principles must also concede that slavery was part and parcel of those Biblical and Christian principles.

It is not necessary to attribute the founding of the nation to the Bible or an organized Christian effort. Any review of the actual history of the founding of the United States, absent spiritualized narratives, shows that highly educated and brilliant men were responsible for debating, working, and creating the founding philosophies and documents. All the Framers were informed by their education, experiences, and faith. They were also informed by selfish motivations and economic interests.

Below is a Summary of the Framers:

Almost all of the 55 Framers had taken part in the Revolution, with at least 29 having served in the Continental forces, most in positions of command. All but two or three had served in colonial or state government during their careers. The vast majority (about 75%) of the delegates were or had been members of the Confederation Congress, and many had been members of the Continental Congress during the Revolution. 25 had been state governors.

More than half of the delegates had trained as lawyers (several had even been judges), although only about a quarter had practiced law as their principal means of business. Others were merchants, manufacturers, shippers, land speculators, bankers or financiers. Several were physicians or small farmers, and one was a minister.

---

[30]   Ibid

Of the 25 who owned slaves, 16 depended on slave labor to run the plantations or other businesses that formed the mainstay of their income. Most of the delegates were landowners with substantial holdings, and most, except for Roger Sherman and William Few, were very comfortably wealthy. George Washington and Robert Morris were among the wealthiest men in the entire country.

Of the 55 Framers, only one was a Christian minister. Regarding the religious faith of the Framers: Of the 55 delegates to the 1787 Constitutional Convention, 28 were Anglicans, 21 were other Protestants, and two were Roman Catholics (D. Carroll and Fitzsimons). Among the Protestant delegates to the Constitutional Convention, eight were Presbyterians, seven were Congregationalists, two were Lutherans, two were Dutch Reformed, and two were Methodists. A few prominent Founding Fathers were anti-clerical notably Jefferson. [31]

It is a reach of imagination and romanticism to believe the 55 Framers acted as a group of Christians in consultation with the Scriptures and prayer. The work of the Framers, as is the case with most good work owes to the skill of the persons working, whether Christian or non-Christian.

One very significant factor argues against the rosy Christian nationalist perspective about our nation's founding: **SLAVERY**.

For many of us, celebrating our nation's founding as a triumph of the Bible and Christianity is offensive given the treatment and property status of our ancestors. To be sure, the formation of the United States, developing the governing documents, and organizing independent colonies was a triumph of human enterprise and self-governing. The telling of history cannot overlook owning, selling, and abusing humans

---

[31]   Lambert, Franklin T. (2003). *The Founding Fathers and the Place of Religion in America.* Princeton, New Jersey: Princeton University Press.

in the service of other humans used to build their economy was decidedly ungodly. It was not something Jesus would have done.

The historic facts regarding the formation of the nation are compelling reading without the hyperbole of a Christian nationalist narrative. The facts are far more interesting than the fabrications.

Formation of the United States

The first Continental Congress met in Carpenter's Hall in Philadelphia, from September 5, to October 26, 1774. All of the colonies except Georgia sent delegates. These were elected by the people, by the colonial legislatures, or by the committees of correspondence of the respective colonies. The colonies presented there were united in a determination to show their combined authority to Great Britain.[32]

The objective of the first Continental Congress was not to declare independence from Great Britain, which some desired to do, but to work on issues related to their relationship and dealings with Great Britain. Due to policies imposed upon them, living under the authority of Great Britain and King George III became untenable.

The Second Continental Congress convened on May 10, 1775 with representatives from 12 of the 13 colonies in Philadelphia shortly after the Battles of Lexington and Concord. The Second Congress functioned as a de facto national government at the outset of the Revolutionary War. All thirteen colonies were represented by the time Congress adopted the Lee Resolution which declared independence from Britain on July 2, 1776.[33] The Declaration was a formal explanation of why Congress had voted to declare independence from Great Britain, more than a year after the outbreak of the American Revolutionary War. The Declaration of Independence was adopted by the Second Continental Congress meeting in Philadelphia, Pennsylvania, on July 4, 1776.

---

[32] *First Continental Congress.* (2020). Independence Hall Association. https://www.ushistory.org/declaration/related/congress.html

[33] Wikipedia contributors. (2020). *Second Continental Congress.* Wikipedia. https://en.m.wikipedia.org/wiki/Second_Continental_Congress

The American Revolutionary War (1775–1783), also known as the American War of Independence, was initiated by the thirteen original colonies against the Kingdom of Great Britain over their objection to Parliament's direct taxation and its lack of colonial representation.[34] The Revolutionary War was won in 1781 with the help of the French.

Following the war, the Constitutional Convention was convened to work on the United States Constitution. The Bill of Rights were the first ten amendments to the completed Constitution, which was finally ratified on June 21, 1788.

For all the wisdom of the Constitution, it is my view that the Framers should have abolished slavery when the nation was founded. This would have been the Christian thing to do, notwithstanding the extreme difficulty in doing so.

The profitability of slavery, dependence on slave labor by 16 of the Framers, and the nation's economic interests outweighed applying Biblical principles. By 1789, five of the Northern states started to gradually abolish slavery. Early Americans should have also dealt justly with Native Americans.

Failing to end slavery as a nation resulted in a future of immense misery, division, and suffering leading to the Civil War with 618,222 deaths as Americans maimed and killed one another.

As a candidate for the US Senate, Abraham Lincoln gave a remarkable, and prophetic, speech in Springfield, Illinois on June 16, 1858 in which he said:

> "A house divided against itself, cannot stand." I believe this government cannot endure permanently half slave and half free. I do not expect the Union to be dissolved — I do not expect the house to fall — but I do expect it will cease to be divided. It will become all one thing or all the other.

---

[34] Wikipedia contributors. (2020). *American Revolutionary War*. Wikipedia. https://en.m.wikipedia.org/wiki/American_Revolutionary_War

The rise of Christian-sanctioned white supremacy in the 19th and 20th centuries (through theological justifications offered by the Southern Baptist Convention and other pro-slavery theologians),[35] and instances of domestic terrorism against Black people by groups such as the Ku Klux Klan were a blight on the 20th Century. Bigotry against, and false narratives about, African Americans continue to the present day.

Dr. Carter G. Woodson wrote with keen insight long ago, in 1930;

> By their peculiar "reasoning," too, theologians have sanctioned most of the ills of the ages. They justified the Inquisition, serfdom, and slavery. Theologians of our time defend segregation and the annihilation of one race by the other. They have drifted away from righteousness into an effort to make wrong seem to be right.[36]

None of the preceding facts argue in favor of a nation established on Biblical or Christian principles, especially if one believes Jesus Christ as the core of "Christian principles." Acknowledgement of the truth about our nation's history is a key component to genuine racial reconciliation.

---

[35] Jones, Robert P.. *White Too Long: The Legacy of White Supremacy in American Christianity* (p. 34). Simon & Schuster. Kindle Edition.

[36] Woodson, Carter, G. 1933 *The Mis-Education of the Negro* (p. 43). Kindle Edition.

Reflection Questions

1. What is the best case that America was founded as a Christian nation?

2. What are arguments against America being founded as a Christian nation?

3. How could Christians be slave owners? What was the justification?

4. Why were Black people not accepted as United States citizens?

5. Where does the Constitution approve or forbid treating persons as slaves?

6. What was the consequence of slavery becoming a part of the founding of the United States?

7. What Scriptural and social justice action can we employ to help in the above issue?

CHAPTER 6

~

Christianity v. Christ

"Shallow understanding from people of good will is more frustrating than absolute misunderstanding from people of ill will. Lukewarm acceptance is much more bewildering than outright rejection." (Rev. Dr. Martin Luther King, *The Letter from the Birmingham Jail*)

Is the United States a Christian nation? There is no question that people who identify as Christian are the predominant religious group in the United States. A Pew Research study in 2019 stated that 65% of Americans identify as Christians.[37] By that metric, the United States can indeed identify as a Christian nation. That same study also identified a decline in people who identify as Christians.

Both Protestantism and Catholicism are experiencing losses of population share. Currently, 43% of U.S. adults identify with Protestantism, down from 51% in 2009. And one-in-five adults (20%) are Catholic, down from 23% in 2009. Meanwhile, all subsets of the religiously unaffiliated population – a group also known as religious "nones" – have seen their numbers swell.[38]

---

[37] *Decline of Christianity Continues at Rapid Pace.* (2019). Pew Research Center's Religion & Public Life Project. https://www.pewforum.org/2019/10/17/in-u-s-decline-of-christianity-continues-at-rapid-pace/

[38] Ibid.

Those who understand Biblical truth and the reality of the New Birth in Christ know that all 65% of Americans who identify as Christians could not be followers of the Lord Jesus Christ. Self identifying as a Christian and actually being a follower of Jesus are not the same thing. Many of us have the personal experience of having called ourselves Christians when we did not live in communion with Christ, obey the Scriptures, or serve God. A survey question that asks, "Are you a Christian" elicits an easy answer without qualification. As a brand, "Christian" may be unpopular to many. To differentiate between nominal and real Christians we use terms such as "born-again Christian" or "Spirit filled Christian."

The decline of people who identify as Christians does not necessarily indicate that there are fewer Christians, whether born again or in name only. It could indicate that people have chosen not to identify with Christianity for reasons such as disdain for the poor example of those who call themselves Christians, disappointment with the alignment of Christians with partisan politics, or other factors that poorly reflect on Christianity as a "brand." No reasonable person expects all of those who say they are Christian to be authentic, but high profile examples of compromised and evil persons disparage the concept of a Christian.

Dylann Roof, an avowed white supremacist, and a Christian, plotted, shot, and killed nine African Americans at their church in Charleston, South Carolina. His was not an act of insanity, but a pre-meditated murder based on long held beliefs about the perceived wrongs that Black people have perpetuated against American society. He stated:

> "I would like to make it crystal clear, I do not regret what I did," Roof wrote. "I am not sorry. I have not shed a tear for the innocent people I killed." [39]

---

[39] Shah, C. (2017, January 6). *Dylann Roof diary: "I am not sorry."* CNN. https://edition.cnn.com/2017/01/05/us/dylann-roof-trial/index.html

Roof's twisted and demonic worldview is clearly not associated with Christ or the teachings of the Word of God, however, **Christianity is no barrier to brutality**. Being baptized, a church member in good standing, with regular church attendance growing up did nothing to help him. In reality, his form of empty Christianity made him worse.

> Although it received little press and was rarely incorporated into explanations of his motivations, Dylann Roof's identity as a white Christian was central to his worldview. As he became more radicalized by contact with white supremacist websites, reading materials, and organizations, the evidence suggests that his Christian identity easily accommodated this shift. At the time he committed the murders, Roof was a baptized member in good standing at St. Paul's Lutheran Church in Columbia, a church associated with the Evangelical Lutheran Church in America (ELCA), a white mainline Protestant denomination. According to his stepmother, Roof regularly went to church growing up, including catechism classes. (Robert P. Jones)[40]

Religious Christianity that lacks a genuine relationship with Christ can be worse than living as a non-religious sinner. Self-deception is perilous, especially when one believes he knows and serves God when he does neither. Human pride combined with religious deception can result in holding "convictions" with no basis in Christ or in scriptural truth. Self-deception, inauthentic Christianity, and religious conviction can be a lethal combination.

The Shifting Values of Conservative Christians

Only weeks after "Bloody Sunday" in Selma, Alabama on March 7, 1965 during which peaceful protesters who crossed the Edmund Pettus Bridge were beaten by State Troopers, Rev. Jerry Falwell gave his response during a sermon;

---

[40] Jones, Robert P.. *White Too Long: The Legacy of White Supremacy in American Christianity* (p. 139). Simon & Schuster. Kindle Edition.

"Believing the Bible as I do, I would find it impossible to stop preaching the pure saving gospel of Jesus Christ and begin doing anything else—including the fighting of Communism, or participating in the civil rights reform... Preachers are not called to be politicians, but to be soul winners."[41]

This was the position of many conservative Christians of the era, including those who opposed the efforts of Dr. King, the Civil Rights movement, and the pursuit of Black Americans seeking equal rights. By the 1970's, Jerry Falwell reversed course and stated;

"The idea that religion and politics don't mix was invented by the Devil to keep Christians from running their own country."[42]

Jerry Falwell started the *Moral Majority* in 1979 which began a trend of Evangelical Christians using political action and government authority to achieve the aim of *"running the country."* The organization disbanded in 1989.[43] The movement's greatest achievement culminated in helping elect Donald J. Trump to the presidency in 2016, a man without governing experience, lacking moral character, but compliant to the wishes of religious leaders. 81% of Evangelical Christians supported his candidacy. A similar percentage supported his presidency, and by association, endorsed his poor character. The Civil Rights movement of the 1950s and 1960s did not make the mistake of becoming politically partisan. They exercised their Christian influence in society and upon government using appropriate Biblical justice and social justice methodology.

This era of American history will be remembered as unBiblical compromise in the service of political power to bring America *"Back from the Brink"* in the words of one of the politically motivated Christ-

---

[41] Jones, Robert P.. *White Too Long: The Legacy of White Supremacy in American Christianity* (p. 103). Simon & Schuster. Kindle Edition.

[42] Ibid.

[43] *Moral Majority | Definition*, History, Mission, & Facts. Encyclopedia Britannica. https://www.britannica.com/topic/Moral-Majority

ian groups during the 2020 election cycle.[44] These actions are an illustration of the phrase, *"The Ends Justify the Means,"* and represents a departure of the Biblically focused Evangelical movement of the early 20th century. Spiritual renewal and revival was the focus of the past. Today the focus is more on forming political alliances and working to Christianize government.

Frederick Douglass, In His Words

It should also be noted that many slave owners in the 18th and 19th Centuries claimed to be Christians. Frederick Douglass, in his autobiography, reports that Christian slave owners could be especially brutal.

Master Thomas at length said he would stand it no longer. I had lived with him nine months, during which time he had given me a number of severe whippings, all to no good purpose. He resolved to put me out, as he said, to be broken; and, for this purpose, he let me for one year to a man named Edward Covey. Mr. Covey was a poor man, a farm-renter. He rented the place upon which he lived, as also the hands with which he tilled it. Mr. Covey had acquired a very high reputation for breaking young slaves, and this reputation was of immense value to him. It enabled him to get his farm tilled with much less expense to himself than he could have had it done without such a reputation. Some slaveholders thought it not much loss to allow Mr. Covey to have their slaves one year, for the sake of the training to which they were subjected, without any other compensation. He could hire young help with great ease, in consequence of this reputation. Added to the natural good qualities of Mr. Covey, he was a professor of religion--a pious soul--a member and a class-leader in the Methodist church. All of this added weight to his reputation as a "nigger-breaker." I was aware of all the facts,

---

44 America On the Brink. (2020, October 1). Truth & Liberty Coalition. https://truthandliberty.net/voteyourvalues

having been made acquainted with them by a young man who had lived there. (Frederick Douglass)[45]

Douglass further wrote:

Revivals of religion and revivals in the slave-trade go hand in hand together. The slave prison and the church stand near each other. The clanking of fetters and the rattling of chains in the prison, and the pious psalm and solemn prayer in the church, may be heard at the same time. The dealer in the bodies and souls of men ... gives his blood-stained gold to support the pulpit, and the pulpit, in return, covers his infernal business with the garb of Christianity. (Frederick Douglass) [46]

Claiming to be "Christian," on its face, is meaningless. It has become my practice to identify as a "Christ Follower." This term keeps me in the mind of following the Lord Jesus Christ and not just identifying with an organization or movement. We may do better by adopting a relational approach to living out our faith, rather than a transactional approach. Relating to the person of Christ through the Holy Spirit, in line with the Scriptures, is better than claiming a label and doing superficial works to show our worthiness. The former requires a relationship with God, while the latter only requires a religion.

The words of Jesus are the final reality:

"For a good tree does not bear bad fruit, nor does a bad tree bear good fruit. For every tree is known by its own fruit. For men do not gather figs from thorns, nor do they gather grapes from a bramble bush. A good man out of the good treasure of his heart brings forth good; and an evil man out of the evil treasure of his heart brings forth evil. For out of the abundance of the heart his mouth speaks." (Luke 6:43-45 NKJV)

---

[45] Douglass, F. (1845). *Narrative of the Life of Frederick Douglass, an American Slave. Written by Himself.* University of North Carolina at Chapel Hill. https://docsouth.unc.edu/neh/douglass/douglass.html

[46] Ibid.

These disturbing instances of false Christians cannot diminish the reality of the immense amount of good and godly work done by followers of Jesus Christ. Nor can these horrendous examples simply be attributed to "bad apples" among genuine Christians. For every bad apple there are too many "good apples" who lacked discernment, looked the other way, or failed to respond to indications of someone practicing inauthentic faith. There is also the structural problem within Christianity where Christians do not actively resist white supremacy and racial injustice. Too many hold the view racial injustices are troubles in the past and we should just move on. Yes, it would be good to move on from the past, except for mindsets and behaviors that continue into the present day. It is not enough to view racism is wrong, one must become actively anti-racist, by holding persons accountable who exhibit poor behaviors as it relates to minorities, and be proactive in identifying and addressing ongoing patterns of systemic racism. We can do better.

Reflection Questions

1. What is a Christian? How can this be proven?

2. What was within white supremacy and aberrant Christianity that motivated Dylann Roof to hate and kill Black people?

3. Why must Christians actively resist white supremacy and racial injustice?

4. As a practice of social justice, how did the Moral Majority fall short, where the Civil Rights movement succeeded?

5. What Scriptural and social justice action can we employ to help with issues raised in this chapter?

CHAPTER 7

~

Dr. King's Concept of Justice and the Role of the Church

Commentary on Dr. King's "Letter from the Birmingham Jail"

M any of the answers we seek do not come from new places. Some of the best concepts and insights come from an old place.

In April 1963, Martin Luther King was jailed in Birmingham, Alabama, after he defied a state court's injunction and led a march of Black protesters without a permit, urging an Easter boycott of white-owned stores. A statement published in The Birmingham News, written by eight moderate white clergymen, criticized the march and other demonstrations. This prompted King to write a lengthy response, begun in the margins of the newspaper. He smuggled it out with the help of his lawyer, and the nearly 7,000 words were transcribed. (From the Atlantic Magazine)[47]

At 34 years of age, his words were a masterpiece of making an argument in favor of a cause. This letter shows Dr. King's clarity about injustice, understanding of equal justice, love of country, powers of logic, grasp of Scripture, boldness, humility, and much more. In this chapter I will highlight passages that continue to be relevant and instructive to our 21st Century challenges. This is not an analysis or expo-

---

[47]   King, M. L. (1933). *Letter From Birmingham Jail. The Atlantic.* https://www.theatlantic.com/magazine/archive/2018/02/letter-from-a-birmingham-jail/552461/

sition of the letter. These are my reflections on portions of the words and concepts written by Dr. King.

PREPARING TO RESPOND

KING: I came across your recent statement calling my present activities "unwise and untimely." Seldom do I pause to answer criticism of my work and ideas...But since I feel that you are men of genuine good will and that your criticisms are sincerely set forth, I want to try to answer your statement in what I hope will be patient and reasonable terms.

Opponents of equal justice have reasoned their way to justifications for what they do. Whether slave owners of the 19th Century, segregationists of the 20th Century, or white supremacists of the 21st Century, opponents to justice have an intellectual basis for their actions. Too often, that basis is informed by bigotry and bad theology. Dr. King stated "I want to try to answer your statement." In reality, he didn't "try." His words were a "tour de force" of reason and logic.

In our day of some protests lacking discipline and clear purpose, Dr. King and the activists of his era used their intellect to overcome the reasoning of opponents to equal justice. He believed that people of "good will" could be persuaded by sound arguments. We should believe the same. When people of good will know better, they can do better.

NOT ONE MAN, AN INEVITABLE FORCE FOR CHANGE

KING: We have some eighty-five affiliated organizations across the South, and one of them is the Alabama Christian Movement for Human Rights. Frequently we share staff, educational and financial resources with our affiliates. Several months ago the affiliate here in Birmingham asked us to be on call to engage in a nonviolent direct action program if such were deemed necessary. We readily consented, and when the hour came we lived up to our promise. So I, along with several members of my staff, am here because I was invited here. I am here because I have organizational ties here.

Dr. King showed that he was not acting alone. He was part of a large and highly organized organism of capable, like-minded persons. Putting him in jail did not stop the movement. It didn't even slow it down. He presented a case of inevitability to his fellow ministers. He made them understand that they were dealing with a force for inevitable change not just the actions of a young preacher and a few angry people.

In the spring of 2020, during the wake of the murder of George Floyd, protests happened all across the nation and world. Unfortunately, too many peaceful protests ended in rioting, which hurt the credibility of the protests. We know that some of the rioters were outsiders coming into cities to disrupt peaceful protests. Many of these actions contributed to a false narrative that protests were essentially riots caused by Black Lives Matter participants and African Americans. This was the objective of those who infiltrated peaceful protests to introduce violence and destruction of property[48]. As a result, many of the effective, organized, peaceful protests were overlooked by the media in favor of more "newsworthy" violent acts.

One of the persons and movements in the United States who has followed the model of the successful Civil Rights Movement era is Rev. Dr. William J. Barber II and the Repairers of the Breach organization (www.breachrepairers.org) based in Goldsboro, North Carolina.

PRINCIPLES OF ACTION

KING: In any nonviolent campaign there are four basic steps: collection of the facts to determine whether injustices exist; negotiation; self purification; and direct action. We have gone through all these steps in Birmingham. There can be no gainsaying the fact that racial injustice engulfs this community. Birmingham is probably the most thoroughly segregated city in the United States. Its ugly record of brutality is widely known. Negroes have experienced

---

[48] MacFarquhar, N. (2020). *Many Claim Extremists Are Sparking Protest Violence. But Which Extremists?* New York Times. https://www.nytimes.com/2020/05/31/us/george-floyd-protests-white-supremacists-antifa.html

grossly unjust treatment in the courts. There have been more un-solved bombings of Negro homes and churches in Birmingham than in any other city in the nation.

Dr. King made it known that they were governed by principles, not emotions. He demonstrated rational action in the face of irrational treatment.

He listed four steps to a non-violent campaign:

1. Collection of the facts to determine whether injustices exist

2. Negotiation

3. Self purification

4. Direct action

The item "self-purification" is interesting. The King Center pub-lished a "Glossary of Non-Violence" on their website.[49] "Purification" is defined as *"The cleansing of anger, selfishness and violent attitudes from the heart and soul in preparation for a nonviolent struggle."* This is another indication of the depth of preparation that was built into their actions. Protest organizers today should study Dr. King's methodology and discipline.

A NETWORK OF MUTUALITY

KING: Moreover, I am cognizant of the interrelatedness of all communities and states. I cannot sit idly by in Atlanta and not be concerned about what happens in Birmingham. Injustice any-where is a threat to justice everywhere. We are caught in an in-escapable network of mutuality, tied in a single garment of destiny. Whatever affects one directly, affects all indirectly. Never again can we afford to live with the narrow, provincial "outside agitator" idea. Anyone who lives inside the United States can never be considered an outsider anywhere within its bounds.

---

[49] *Glossary of Nonviolence*. (2019). The King Center. https://thekingcenter.org/glossary-of-nonviolence/

Dr. King tied the actions of himself and the movement to *"an in-escapable network of mutuality, tied in a single garment of destiny."* In this, he showed how his audience of clergymen were either part of the answer or part of the problem. In addressing the accusation of his being an "outsider," King appealed to their sense of nationalism and patriotism with the words, *"Anyone who lives inside the United States can never be considered an outsider anywhere within its bounds."* He probably caused many to reach for their dictionaries to understand the words he used!

PHILOSOPHICAL FOUNDATION

KING: You may well ask: "Why direct action? Why sit ins, marches and so forth? Isn't negotiation a better path?" ...Just as Socrates felt that it was necessary to create a tension in the mind so that individuals could rise from the bondage of myths and half truths to the unfettered realm of creative analysis and objective appraisal, so must we see the need for nonviolent gadflies to create the kind of tension in society that will help men rise from the dark depths of prejudice and racism to the majestic heights of understanding and brotherhood. The purpose of our direct action program is to create a situation so crisis packed that it will inevitably open the door to negotiation.

Dr. King appealed to the formal training of the ministers, many of whom were highly educated. By citing Socrates, he used the art of Philosophy to present the philosophical underpinnings of their strategy. He revealed to them that creating "tension" was part of their plan to "open the door" to negotiation. In this, Dr. King showed transparency. He gave people of "good will" every reason to support his efforts. It was a remarkable strategy! It seems that we have much to learn today from the movement 57 years later.

WHY WE WON'T WAIT

KING: For years now I have heard the word "Wait!" It rings in the ear of every Negro with piercing familiarity. This "Wait" has almost always meant "Never." We must come to see, with one of our distinguished jurists, that "justice too long delayed is justice denied." We have waited for more than 340 years for our constitutional and God given rights. The nations of Asia and Africa are moving with jetlike speed toward gaining political independence, but we still creep at horse and buggy pace toward gaining a cup of coffee at a lunch counter. Perhaps it is easy for those who have never felt the stinging darts of segregation to say, "Wait." But when you have seen vicious mobs lynch your mothers and fathers at will and drown your sisters and brothers at whim; when you have seen hate filled policemen curse, kick and even kill your Black brothers and sisters; when you see the vast majority of your twenty million Negro brothers smothering in an airtight cage of poverty in the midst of an affluent society; when you suddenly find your tongue twisted and your speech stammering as you seek to explain to your six year old daughter why she can't go to the public amusement park that has just been advertised on television, and see tears welling up in her eyes when she is told that Funtown is closed to colored children.

Regarding the assertion that Black people should "wait" for a better time for action or wait for conditions to improve, Dr. King offered impassioned words and personally challenged the clergyman to view Black people as neglected "brothers," a common term among followers of Christ. He wrote, *"You see the vast majority of your twenty million Negro brothers smothering in an airtight cage of poverty."* At this point in the letter, he used the words "you" and "yours" to engage and implicate the clergymen in his arguments. He made injustice and brutality an experience for the readers.

TWO KINDS OF LAWS

KING: There comes a time when the cup of endurance runs over, and men are no longer willing to be plunged into the abyss of despair. I hope, sirs, you can understand our legitimate and unavoidable impatience. You express a great deal of anxiety over our willingness to break laws. This is certainly a legitimate concern. Since we so diligently urge people to obey the Supreme Court's decision of 1954 outlawing segregation in the public schools, at first glance it may seem rather paradoxical for us consciously to break laws. One may well ask: "How can you advocate breaking some laws and obeying others?" The answer lies in the fact that there are two types of laws: just and unjust. I would be the first to advocate obeying just laws. One has not only a legal but a moral responsibility to obey just laws. Conversely, one has a moral responsibility to disobey unjust laws. I would agree with St. Augustine that "an unjust law is no law at all."

Dr. King addressed legal mandates and explained his philosophy of civil disobedience. He answered the question: *"How can you advocate breaking some laws and obeying others?"* King outlined two types of laws: "just and unjust." He advocated the importance of being law abiding citizens in affirmation of the conscience of his "law and order" readers. He also subtly reminded them that many whites disobeyed the 1954 Supreme Court decision Brown v. Board of Education that mandated the desegregation of schools—a "just" law that many whites disobeyed.

King made a powerful argument, "One has not only a legal but a moral responsibility to obey just laws. Conversely, one has a moral responsibility to disobey unjust laws. I would agree with St. Augustine that 'an unjust law is no law at all.'"

UNJUST LAWS DAMAGE THE SOUL

KING: All segregation statutes are unjust because segregation distorts the soul and damages the personality. It gives the segregator a false sense of superiority and the segregated a false sense of inferiority.

In addition to addressing the injustice of segregation, he also highlighted the psychological damage caused by it. Not only damage to the person being segregated, but damage to the person perpetrating the injustice through a false sense of superiority. It is not rational for one person to feel superior to another person when God made all people in His image and likeness.

DISMANTLING INJUSTICE ARGUMENTS

KING: Who can say that the legislature of Alabama which set up that state's segregation laws was democratically elected? Throughout Alabama all sorts of devious methods are used to prevent Negroes from becoming registered voters, and there are some counties in which, even though Negroes constitute a majority of the population, not a single Negro is registered. Can any law enacted under such circumstances be considered democratically structured?

In his letter, Dr. King continued to dismantle arguments favoring injustice against Black people. He pointed out that some counties in Alabama had majority Black populations and none were registered to vote, which was a clear outcome of racist injustice. He continued to appeal to the conscience and sense of fairness on the part of the White clergy. Again, he appealed to those of "good will."

GENUINE LAW AND ORDER

KING: I hope you are able to see the distinction I am trying to point out. In no sense do I advocate evading or defying the law, as would the rabid segregationist. That would lead to anarchy. One who breaks an unjust law must do so openly, lovingly, and with a willingness to accept the penalty. I submit that an individual who breaks a law that conscience tells him is unjust, and who willingly accepts the penalty of imprisonment in order to arouse the conscience of the community over its injustice, is in reality expressing the highest respect for law.

Dr. King fully understood the importance of a society based on law and order in guarding against anarchy. He expressed his understanding and respect for the law and taking responsibility for actions against "unjust laws." After all, he was sitting in a jail writing a letter as personal proof of that concept!

EXAMPLES OF CIVIL DISOBEDIENCE

KING: Of course, there is nothing new about this kind of civil disobedience. It was evidenced sublimely in the refusal of Shadrach, Meshach and Abednego to obey the laws of Nebuchadnezzar, on the ground that a higher moral law was at stake. It was practiced superbly by the early Christians, who were willing to face hungry lions and the excruciating pain of chopping blocks rather than submit to certain unjust laws of the Roman Empire. To a degree, academic freedom is a reality today because Socrates practiced civil disobedience. In our own nation, the Boston Tea Party represented a massive act of civil disobedience.

He appealed to the clergymen using Scriptural and historical examples of civil disobedience by the Hebrews and Christians. Dr. King then "dropped the mic" with reminding the White clergymen that the United States itself was founded on acts of civil disobedience such as the Boston Tea Party. This was a political protest that occurred on December 16, 1773, at Griffin's Wharf in Boston, Massachusetts. American colonists, frustrated and angry at Britain for imposing "taxation without representation," (illegally) dumped 342 chests of tea imported by the British East India Company into the harbor. [50]

THE SACRIFICES OF LEADERS

KING: Was not Paul an extremist for the Christian gospel: "I bear in my body the marks of the Lord Jesus." Was not Martin Luther an extremist: "Here I stand; I cannot do otherwise, so help me God." And John Bunyan: "I will stay in jail to the end of my days before I make a butchery of my conscience." And Abraham Lincoln: "This nation cannot survive half slave and half free." And Thomas Jefferson: "We hold these truths to be self evident, that all

---

[50] History.com Editors. (2020). *Boston Tea Party*. History Channel. https://www.history.com/topics/american-revolution/boston-tea-party

men are created equal..." So the question is not whether we will be extremists, but what kind of extremists we will be. Will we be extremists for hate or for love? Will we be extremists for the preservation of injustice or for the extension of justice? In that dramatic scene on Calvary's hill three men were crucified. We must never forget that all three were crucified for the same crime--the crime of extremism. Two were extremists for immorality, and thus fell below their environment. The other, Jesus Christ, was an extremist for love, truth and goodness, and thereby rose above his environment.

Dr. King wrote about the sacrifices of people who dedicated their lives to making other lives better. He cited the Apostle Paul, the reformer Martin Luther (his own namesake), John Bunyan, Abraham Lincoln, Thomas Jefferson, and the Lord Jesus Christ! It was a powerful flourish by a preacher communicating to preachers.

MARTIN LUTHER KING, THE PASTOR

KING: I have traveled the length and breadth of Alabama, Mississippi and all the other southern states. On sweltering summer days and crisp autumn mornings I have looked at the South's beautiful churches with their lofty spires pointing heavenward. I have beheld the impressive outlines of her massive religious education buildings. Over and over I have found myself asking: "What kind of people worship here? Who is their God? Where were their voices when the lips of Governor Barnett dripped with words of interposition and nullification? Where were they when Governor Wallace gave a clarion call for defiance and hatred? Where were their voices of support when bruised and weary Negro men and women decided to rise from the dark dungeons of complacency to the bright hills of creative protest?"

Yes, these questions are still in my mind. In deep disappointment I have wept over the laxity of the church. But be assured that my tears have been tears of love. There can be no deep disappointment where there is not deep love. Yes, I love the church. How could I do otherwise? I am in the rather unique position of being the son, the grandson and the great grandson of preachers. Yes, I see the church as the body of Christ. But, oh! How we have blemished and scarred that body through social neglect and through fear of being nonconformists.

Martin Luther King, the Pastor, issued an indictment against the church. I cannot envision how a pastor could have read those words and not have been moved. This part of the letter presents the most emotional words of his text. He wrote, *"In deep disappointment I have wept over the laxity of the church. But be assured that my tears have been tears of love. There can be no deep disappointment where there is not deep love."*

This was a clear expression of a follower and servant of Christ looking at the broken state of the church in his day. It seems that brokenness is present to this day.

USING CHRIST TO HINDER FELLOW CHRISTIANS

KING: I have just received a letter from a white brother in Texas. He writes: "All Christians know that the colored people will receive equal rights eventually, but it is possible that you are in too great a religious hurry. It has taken Christianity almost two thousand years to accomplish what it has. The teachings of Christ take time to come to earth."

It was quite audacious for someone to send a letter justifying the delay of justice to people and believers in Christ using Christ to argue against receiving His blessing. Whatever this person's reasoning, he certainly showed no respect to the teachings of the Bible and of Christ. I'm reminded of Hebrews 11 which reads, "Now faith is the substance of things hope for and the evidence of things not seen."

From Matthew 4:17, The scripture reads, *"From that time Jesus began to preach and say, "Repent, for the kingdom of heaven is at hand."*

"Now faith" and "the Kingdom of heaven is at hand" is not something one has to wait 2000 years to receive, or receive "eventually."

LOSS OF AUTHENTICITY FOR THE AMERICAN CHURCH

KING: But the judgment of God is upon the church as never before. If today's church does not recapture the sacrificial spirit of the early church, it will lose its authenticity, forfeit the loyalty of millions, and be dismissed as an irrelevant social club with no meaning for the twentieth century. Every day I meet young people whose disappointment with the church has turned into outright disgust.

Dr. King possessed the insight and foresight to know that the unrighteous actions of the church in his era damaged the church's credibility with unchurched young people. His words were prophetic. The same loss of authenticity occurs today with millennials who observe ministers aligning with political power brokers for personal gain and not for the benefit of people in society.

LOOKING FOR THE "CHURCH WITHIN THE CHURCH

KING: Is organized religion too inextricably bound to the status quo to save our nation and the world? Perhaps I must turn my faith to the inner spiritual church, the church within the church, as the true ekklesia and the hope of the world. But again I am thankful to God that some noble souls from the ranks of organized religion have broken loose from the paralyzing chains of conformity and joined us as active partners in the struggle for freedom. They have left their secure congregations and walked the streets of Albany, Georgia, with us. They have gone down the highways of the South on tortuous rides for freedom. Yes, they have gone to jail with us. Some have been dismissed from their churches, have lost the support of their bishops and fellow ministers. But they have acted in the faith that right defeated is stronger than evil triumphant.

In this part of the letter, Dr. King provided examples where White ministers took a godly stand against injustice and racism. This would seem to be a challenge to the clergy readers of his letter. The courage of many White Americans is not in question. We have seen them sacrifice as much as Black people for a cause that was not to their personal benefit. Many of the Freedom Riders, marchers, and protesters were courageous White and Jewish men and women.

OPPRESSION CANNOT CONTINUE

KING: Oppressed people cannot remain oppressed forever. The yearning for freedom eventually manifests itself, and that is what has happened to the American Negro. Something within has reminded him of his birthright of freedom, and something without has reminded him that it can be gained.

King showed the humanity and equal value of Black Americans. King expounded on the innate yearning for freedom that all humans possess, something they had in common with their White brethren, including the ministers who read the letter.

CONFIDENCE IN THE PROMISE OF AMERICA

KING: We will reach the goal of freedom in Birmingham and all over the nation, because the goal of America is freedom. Abused and scorned though we may be, our destiny is tied up with America's destiny. Before the pilgrims landed at Plymouth, we were here. Before the pen of Jefferson etched the majestic words of the Declaration of Independence across the pages of history, we were here. For more than two centuries our forebears labored in this country without wages; they made cotton king; they built the homes of their masters while suffering gross injustice and shameful humiliation and yet out of a bottomless vitality they continued to thrive and develop. If the inexpressible cruelties of slavery could not stop us, the opposition we now face will surely fail.

Dr. King had confidence in the promise of America. He understood that the nation was founded on principles of personal freedom, even though that freedom was denied to enslaved Americans. The people of that era kept their eyes on the prize of the Bill of Rights and US Constitution. They determined to claim benefits denied to their ancestors. Black Americans were, and are, far more patriotic than people realize. Not by superficial acts like waving flags or wearing flag print t-shirts. A patriot maintains confidence in his country to do the right thing. In hindsight, looking back 57 years, we see that the people of the civil rights movement were correct, *"the goal of America is freedom."*

Freedom is not a privilege for African-Americans, it is our birthright and we have earned it as well. Free Black labor helped make the country wealthy. King expressed confidence to his fellow clergyman that opposition to freedom would fail.

OPTIMISM IN THE FACE OF DESPAIR

KING: I hope this letter finds you strong in the faith. I also hope that circumstances will soon make it possible for me to meet each of you, not as an integrationist or a civil-rights leader but as a fellow clergyman and a Christian brother. Let us all hope that the dark clouds of racial prejudice will soon pass away and the deep fog of misunderstanding will be lifted from our fear drenched communities, and in some not too distant tomorrow the radiant stars of love and brotherhood will shine over our great nation with all their scintillating beauty.

This marvelous closing, written from a jail, Pauline in tone, and reflected the heart of a follower of Christ and a lover of God's church. In spite of the abuse and neglect on the part of some fellow clergy members, Dr. King was not bitter but hopeful. This letter would have certainly captivated the hearts and minds of ministers of good will.

Reflection Questions

1. What are five things you learned from these excerpts and commentary on *The Letter from the Birmingham Jail?*

2. What Scriptural and social justice action can we employ to help with issues raised in this chapter?

CHAPTER 8

~

May 25, 2020
George Floyd

"Racism is not getting worse, it's getting filmed." ~ Will Smith

The slow, torturous killing of George Floyd on May 25, 2020, by police officer Derek Chauvin was a nightmare for George Floyd, his family, and for anyone who later watched the video.

Floyd's death was no less tragic than Philando Castile, Michael Brown, Terence Crutcher, Eric Garner, Alton Sterling, Oscar Grant, Freddie Gray, Botham Jean, Atatiana Jefferson, Bettie Jones, Trayvon Martin, Laquan McDonald, Tamir Rice, Ahmaud Arbery, Breonna Taylor, Rayshard Brooks, Jacob Blake, and too many other people made in the image and likeness of God. These disrespected persons highlight the importance of the phrase, Black Lives Matter.

At the moment when this statement of human concern (not the promotion of an organization) should have received unanimous adoption, there were people saying, *"No, all lives matter!"* This is an intentional insult towards Black people and trivializing of unjust conditions that affect too many African Americans. We have the capacity to focus on people, nations, police officers, our military, government officials, and others.

As Hurricane Sally tracked towards Mississippi and Louisiana in September 2020, prayers went out for the people and preparations were made. No one said, *"All states matter."* A Facebook post highlighted the stated, *"All lives matter,"* followed by a photograph of a

MAGA Trump hat. We all decide who and what matters or not. Willful ignorance and duplicity are among of the hypocrisies of our culture.

We have seen too many backward triumphs of small-mindedness over the acknowledgment of facts and compassionate action. I have read discussions that moved entirely away from George Floyd's murder toward discussions that Black Lives Matter was a Marxist organization that organized all the riots. This is unhelpful at a time when working together is needed.

The Tragedy of Public Opinion

African Americans have long navigated through the attitudes and preconceived notions of those who filter out logic, facts, and compassion. The excerpts below represent sentiments expressed in anonymous public forums like *Facebook* and *Parlia*.[51]

George Floyd's killing was justified - "The role of the police is to prevent crime and to protect society from dangerous individuals. The police were responding to a call from a concerned shopkeeper when they dealt with George Floyd. While the situation might have spiraled out of control, Derek Chauvin was doing his job. Unfortunately, accidental deaths stemming from police intervention are part and parcel of American society. This is a necessary sacrifice for social stability and functioning democracy."
(**Author Note:** *The phrase "necessary sacrifice" justifies killing "dangerous" people? At the time of his death, Floyd was* **seven years removed** *from his time of incarceration. Chauvin's knee on Floyd's neck for nearly eight minutes was far from accidental)*

George Floyd was a criminal - "George Floyd was a convicted criminal. He had spent five years in jail for robbery and assault, as well as facing court countless other times for crimes ranging from drug handling to theft with a firearm. He was not the innocent victim that mainstream media reports suggest. It is hardly surprising

---

[51] *George Floyd's murder was justified* (2020). Parlia. https://www.parlia.com/a/george-floyds-murder-justified

given this long criminal history, that he was treated with suspicion by police."

The black community has unleashed an anti-white campaign of violence - "Wherever you stand on whether George Floyd's murder was justified is irrelevant. The chaos that has unfolded in its wake is where we should be focusing our attention. Black communities have instigated an anti-white movement under the guise of 'equality and justice'. They are destroying (mostly) white businesses in nightly rampages that leave communities terrified and broken. At the heart of the riots is racist hatred towards whites, which is now playing out in this national campaign."

(Author Note: This is false. It is not an uncommon racist false narrative.)

Of course, we do not overreact to anonymous commenters, but opinions such as these highlight bigoted strands within the fabric of our country. Disdain for Black people comes from well-known factors such as bad child training, mis-education, cultures that foster disrespect, false narratives, and erroneous Christian doctrine, such as Black people being "cursed."

This is all the more reason for Christ Followers to stand up against injustice and practice the disciplines of Biblical justice among themselves to gain more authority to practice social justice within our communities. It is no longer acceptable to simply believe that racism is wrong. We must become anti-racist. We must commit to change the culture, not just "lament."

How to Change a Culture

An article from Harvard Business Review, *Changing Company Culture Requires a Movement, Not a Mandate,* was intended for business leaders, but it speaks to the larger culture of our communities and circles of influence.

But culture change can't be achieved through top-down mandate. It lives in the collective hearts and habits of people and their shared perception of "how things are done around here." Someone with authority can demand compliance, but they can't dictate optimism, trust, conviction, or creativity.

The dominant culture and structure of today's organizations are perfectly designed to produce their current behaviors and outcomes, regardless of whether those outcomes are the ones you want. If your hope is for individuals to act differently, it helps to change their surrounding conditions to be more supportive of the new behaviors, particularly when they are antithetical to the dominant culture.

At IDEO, we believe that the most significant change often comes through social movements, and despite the differences between private enterprises and society, leaders can learn from how these initiators engage and mobilize the masses to institutionalize new societal norms.[52]

The writer suggests a company that desires to change its culture must challenge the "natural behaviors" by the "dominant culture." The writer goes on to suggest that we should **"Change their surrounding conditions to be more supportive of the new behaviors."**

Being Salt (Influence) and Light (Dispel Darkness)

The idea of changing conditions fits within the concept of influence and change articulated by Jesus,

*"You are the salt of the earth; but **if the salt loses its flavor**, how shall it be seasoned? It is then **good for nothing** but to be thrown out and trampled underfoot by men. You are the light of the world. A city that is set on a hill cannot be hidden. 15 Nor do*

---

[52] *Changing Company Culture Requires a Movement, Not a Mandate.* (2017,). Harvard Business Review. https://hbr.org/2017/06/changing-company-culture-requires-a-movement-not-a-mandate

*they light a lamp and put it under a basket, but on a lampstand, and it gives light to all who are in the house. **Let your light so shine** before men, that they may see your good works and glorify your Father in heaven."* (Matthew 5:13-16*)*

Salt represents influence. Light dispels darkness. Before we can change the world (social justice), we must change ourselves (Biblical justice). In too many ways, the failures we see in the larger society reflect failures on the part of those of us who should have been instrumental in bringing godly influence and light. As Jesus said, when the salt loses its flavor (or potency), it becomes "good for nothing."

The deafening silence on the part of too many Christians in the wake of injustice, over many decades, is a reflection of a loss of focus on our responsibilities as influencers and light-bearers. The phenomenon of "white fragility" prevents some persons from engaging in matters dealing with racial injustice,

In 2011, Robin DiAngelo coined the term "white fragility" to describe the disbelieving defensiveness that some white people exhibit when their ideas about race and racism are challenged—and particularly when they feel implicated in white supremacy. She writes, *"It's the defensive reactions so many white people have when our racial worldviews, positions, or advantages are questioned or challenged. For a lot of white people, just suggesting that being white has meaning will trigger a deep, defensive response. And that defensiveness serves to maintain both our comfort and our positions in a racially inequitable society from which we benefit."*[53]

The video of the public murder of George Floyd captivated the attention of the entire nation and world. It even moved the "silent majority" to speak up. *Christianity Today* reported on responses by Evangelical

[53] Waldman, K. (2018). *A Sociologist Examines the "White Fragility" That Prevents White Americans from Confronting Racism.* The New Yorker. https://www.newyorker.com/books/page-turner/a-sociologist-examines-the-white-fragility-that-prevents-white-americans-from-confronting-racism

Christians in June 2020. The messages were earnest, howbeit largely weak, in the wake of George Floyd's killing. As of this writing (October, 2020) it seems the moment has been lost to "business as usual." What was missed was specific challenges to the culture of disdain and hatred against Black people. Those messages and responses included:[54]

- The church has a responsibility to denounce racism

- The church should support peaceful protests occurring in response to Floyd's killing

- There are a couple of indications that pastors are "as open as they've ever been" to addressing racial discrimination. (Some have never been open to addressing racism, so nothing has changed.)

- We need an honest conversation about race. (Actually, we don't need another conversation. We need to be actively anti-racist)

- It is important for church leadership to publicly show support for people of color. (A better choice would be to condemn white supremacist attitudes and hold people accountable)

- Offer sermons that address political topics like "race relations."

- Church leaders are going to have to "lead with humility and with being connected to the thoughts and perceptions" of others.

As researcher Robert P. Jones pointed out, responses on the part of too many Evangelicals are often limited to "lament" without concrete action.

White Christians, and even my own childhood home denomination, are gradually beginning to face the bare fact that white su-

---

[54] Roach, D. (2020,). *Most US Pastors Speak Out in Response to George Floyd's Death.* Christianity Today. https://www.christianitytoday.com/news/2020/june/pastors-george-floyd-racism-church-barna-research.html

premacy has played a role in shaping American Christianity. But they have been too quick to see laments and apologies as the end, rather than the beginning, of a process. They also remain full of contradictions and too quickly avert their gaze when the weighty implications of history require concrete, sustained action in the present. (Robert P. Jones) [55]

A Barna Research report confirmed the long-standing lack of recognition of that America's history of slavery and racism has effects to the present day.

According to Barna data published last year, 42 percent of white Christians said they believe America's history of slavery and racism continues to impact African Americans, and about 1 in 5 pastors (19%) across all ethnic groups said **there's nothing the church should do to respond to America's history of racism.**[56]

What is often missing with these studies is the recognition that the "effects" of slavery on Black people have nothing to do within the DNA or psyche of Black folks (i.e., no "slave mentality"). The effect of America's history of slavery and racism is largely seen in the attitudes and actions of too many White people towards Black people (as well as self-loathing by some Black people who publicly chastise one another). My life experience (as anecdotal evidence) shows that a lot of White people are oblivious to their own attitudes about Black people until something happens like the video of George Floyd's murder by a police officer or public protests that demand their attention. At that point, education (or mis-education), training, and pre-conceived notions inform one's reactions.

Today is the day to live the principles of Biblical justice and practice social justice. Again, justice is doing righteousness.

---

[55] Jones, Robert P.. *White Too Long: The Legacy of White Supremacy in American Christianity* (pp. 53-54). Simon & Schuster. Kindle Edition.

[56] *Half of Practicing Christians Say History of Slavery Still Impacts the U.S.* (2019). Barna Group. https://www.barna.com/research/slavery-still-impacts/

*That we should no longer be children, tossed to and fro and carried about with every wind of doctrine, by the trickery of men, in the cunning craftiness of deceitful plotting, but, **speaking the truth in love,** may grow up in all things into Him who is the head—Christ—from whom the whole body, joined and knit together by what every joint supplies, according to the effective working by which every part does its share, causes growth of the body for the edifying of itself in love.* (Ephesians 4:14-16)

Reflection Questions

1. Why did George Floyd's killing spark outrage like no other, besides the video footage?

2. What drives public opinion against Black people?

3. How can a culture be changed?

4. Why is there a pattern of concern about injustice/disrespect against African Americans rising and falling over time?

5. What Scriptural and social justice action can we employ to help in the above issue?

CHAPTER 9

~

Perceptions, PTSD, Incarceration, & Re-Entry

There are 2.2 million people in the nation's prisons and jails—a 500% increase over the last 40 years, more than any other nation.[57]

Is the USA the most criminal nation in the world? Are African American males pre-disposed to doing criminal acts? A better question may be, do we have a systemic problem with civil justice, sentencing, and is there a lack of reform for non-violent offenders? The data verifies that more Black men are incarcerated, per capita, than other groups. By the same measure, more Black men are arrested and convicted of crimes than other groups. Not surprisingly, then, one scholar has predicted, *"imprisonment will become the most significant factor contributing to the dissolution and breakdown of African American families during the decade of the 1990s."* [58]

Although whites represent the majority of suspects arrested for all crimes, blacks are disproportionately more likely to be arrested relative to their share of the U.S. population. The abandonment of rehabilitation in the prison system has resulted in an erosion of modestly protective norms against cruelty toward prisoners.

---

[57] *Criminal Justice Facts.* (2020). The Sentencing Project. https://www.sentencing-project.org/criminal-justice-facts/

[58] King, A., "The Impact of Incarceration on African American Families: Implications for Practice," Families in Society: The Journal of Contemporary Human Services, 74, 145-153 (1993), p.145.)

Enter the Narratives

- "Black on Black" crime as a blight on every major city.

- 33% of Black people make up the national prison population (while 12% of the national population)[59].

- We've heard about the dissolution of the Black family.

- We've seen the videos of police brutality against Black men.

- There are Black men hanging out on corners with their pants sagging.

- There are articles like: "What's Holding Blacks Back? It's black attitudes, not white racism, that's to blame."[60]

- There are titles like, "Black Males and Social Problems."

- And, "Being Black in America Can Be Hazardous to Your Health"[61]

- And, "Is racism responsible for the problems of Black Americans?"[62]

- And, "Do black Americans commit more crime?"[63]

- And much more...

If I were not an African American man raised in the inner city, son of loving parents, a student of public schools, married for 42 years,

[59] Gramlich, J. (2019). *The gap between the number of blacks and whites in prison is shrinking.* Pew Research Center. https://www.pewresearch.org/fact-tank/2019/04/30/shrinking-gap-between-number-of-blacks-and-whites-in-prison/

[60] *What's Holding Blacks Back?* (2019). City Journal. https://www.city-journal.org/html/what%E2%80%99s-holding-blacks-back-12025.html

[61] Khazan, O. (2020). *Being Black in America Can Be Hazardous to Your Health.* The Atlantic. https://www.theatlantic.com/magazine/archive/2018/07/being-black-in-america-can-be-hazardous-to-your-health/561740/

[62] Williams, W. E. (2020). *Is racism responsible for the problems of Black Americans?* Orange County Register. https://www.ocregister.com/2020/07/29/is-racism-responsible-for-the-problems-of-black-americans/

[63] Worrall, P. (2014). *FactCheck: do black Americans commit more crime? Channel 4 News.* https://www.channel4.com/news/factcheck/factcheck-black-americans-commit-crime

raised four children, surrounded by good relationships, and pastoring an African American church for 38 years, I would think there is something gravely wrong with Black people. Statistics and media reports paint a portrait that Blacks are a "problem people." In the words of Dorothy I. Height, former president of the National Council of Negro Women, *"We are not a problem people, we are people with problems."*[64]

Data, properly gathered and assessed, does not lie. There is no minimizing criminal activity on the part of some Black people (that word "some" is missing from studies, articles, conversations, and news reports). Not all narratives are false, but there is one enormous implied false narrative: ***There is something wrong with Black people, as a people.***

This sentiment is unspoken and largely unprovable, but many African Americans can attest to this sentiment as anecdotal evidence. Nothing else explains being followed, pulled over by police, or watched. All of the data, news reports, narratives (both true and false), puts nearly every black person under suspicion in one way or another. Dark skinned black males (who don't wear a "happy face") are suspected more than others. These statements will seem hyper-sensitive, and that would be an accurate assessment. However, it does not make the statements untrue. Some data lie outside the means of measurement. A person's experiences, feelings or fears cannot be accurately measured. Anecdotal evidence is authentic, howbeit unscientific.

One study that is not regularly seen reports on the attitudes of United States citizens towards African Americans, Black people, or "the blacks," – whichever label one prefers. There was a study conducted by a researcher at Ferris State University, *"Negative Racial Stereotypes*

---

64 Ownby, T. (2018). *Hurting Words: Debating Family Problems in the Twentieth-Century South (New Directions in Southern Studies)* (Illustrated ed.). University of North Carolina Press.

and Their Effect on Attitudes Toward African-Americans."[65] There may be others, but that is not my interest in this chapter. Apart from the actual bad deeds of *some* African Americans, there is not a single statistic or study that accurately describes *all* African Americans. For example, the above title, *"Black Males and Social Problems,"* puts focus on all Black males, of which I am one. It is as if being Black makes one responsible for the actions of other Black people in some way. We don't see this phenomenon with White males. The sentiment seems to go that if any significant percentage of Black males are affected by any negative malady, we must all take notice—or we must all be considered "at risk."

The phenomena of treating Black people (especially Black males) as a monolith is one of the most misleading and harmful effects of our culture.[66] Given the many incidents of mass murders committed by White males, no one (rightly) considers being a White male as a risk factor to becoming a mass murderer, nor are White people expected to be responsible for the actions of other White people.[67]

Negative perceptions about Black people will affect the mindsets and play into the confirmation biases of others, including law enforcement agencies.

Sentencing policies, implicit racial bias, and socioeconomic inequity contribute to racial disparities at every level of the criminal justice system. In 2018, people of color made up 37% of the U.S. population but 67% of the prison population. Overall, African Americans are more likely than white Americans to be arrested; once arrested, they are more likely to be convicted; and once con-

[65] Green, L. (2020). *Negative Racial Stereotypes and Their Effect on Attitudes Toward African-Americans.* Ferris State University - Jim Crow Museum. https://www.ferris.edu/htmls/news/jimcrow/links/essays/vcu.htm

[66] Ray, R. (2020). *Black Americans are not a monolithic group.* The Guardian. https://www.theguardian.com/commentisfree/2020/feb/14/black-americans-are-not-a-monolithic-group-so-stop-treating-us-like-one

[67] *U.S.: mass shootings by race 1982-2019.* (2020). Statista. https://www.statista.com/statistics/476456/mass-shootings-in-the-us-by-shooter-s-race/

victed, they are more likely to face stiff sentences. Black men are six times as likely to be incarcerated as white men and Hispanic men are more than twice as likely to be incarcerated as non-Hispanic white men.[68]

Post-Traumatic Stress Disorder

Nothing can excuse poor choices or poor behavior, but perspective is important. We know about the mental and emotional trauma suffered by victims of disasters, military veterans who faced combat, and victims of crime.

Post-traumatic stress disorder (PTSD) is a mental health condition that's triggered by a terrifying event — either experiencing it or witnessing it. Symptoms may include flashbacks, nightmares and severe anxiety, as well as uncontrollable thoughts about the event.[69] Most people who go through traumatic events may have temporary difficulty adjusting and coping, but with time and good self-care, they usually get better. If the symptoms get worse, last for months or even years, and interfere with your day-to-day functioning, you may have PTSD.

It is certain that people from all walks of life may experience PTSD. I often think about innocent persons, especially youth, who have bad encounters with the police or other authority figures. Being falsely accused arrested, handcuffed, or worse, is a traumatic event––likely much worse than many people can imagine. While less traumatic, being followed or pulled over is stressful. I've been pulled over on occasions and found it disgusting. Nothing went wrong, but I was angry about my time being wasted.

Going forward, there will be a vivid memory of George Floyd being tortured and slowly killed by a police officer that will make me wonder, "What type of cop is this?"

---

[68] Ibid.

[69] *Post-traumatic stress disorder (PTSD) - Symptoms and causes.* (2018). Mayo Clinic. https://www.mayoclinic.org/diseases-conditions/post-traumatic-stress-disorder/symptoms-causes/syc-20355967

Black men are counseled to simply "comply," but when you know injustice is happening, you are in no mood to play along. Of course, we comply, but it is not an occasion for happy talk and smiles. Black men (again, within the monolith narrative) are sometimes criticized for having a "bad attitude," but injustice is not an occasion for a superficial display of a "good attitude." Others placed in the same conditions as Black men would not likely not pass with "flying colors" (I've seen people get frustrated standing in a slow moving line).

As a law abiding citizen and taxpayer, I don't work for the police, they work for me. I appreciate their service and the risks they take, but pulling me over for doing nothing wrong, because I am Black, is not a happy occasion. I will never accept such treatment as normal and part of being a Black man in America.

My experiences do not qualify as a PTSD inducing event, but bad feelings linger. I can only imagine how a Black person may feel who has been violated in a more intense manner. There seems to be a feeling among some cops that it is necessary to be "tough and firm" with Black men, more than with others. Again, this is an anecdotal statement.

You can develop post-traumatic stress disorder when you go through, see or learn about an event involving actual or threatened death, serious injury or sexual violation. After surviving a traumatic event, many people have PTSD-like symptoms at first, such as being unable to stop thinking about what's happened. Fear, anxiety, anger, depression, guilt — all are common reactions to trauma. However, the majority of people exposed to trauma do not develop long-term post-traumatic stress disorder.

Because the effects of trauma on people varies greatly, it is helpful to look at symptoms of Post-traumatic stress disorder. (Taken from the Mayo Clinic website)[70]

---

[70] *Post-traumatic stress disorder (PTSD) - Symptoms and causes.* (2018). Mayo Clinic. https://www.mayoclinic.org/diseases-conditions/post-traumatic-stress-disorder/symptoms-causes/syc-20355967

Intrusive memories

Symptoms of intrusive memories may include:

- Recurrent, unwanted distressing memories of the traumatic event
- Reliving the traumatic event as if it were happening again (flashbacks)
- Upsetting dreams or nightmares about the traumatic event
- Severe emotional distress or physical reactions to something that reminds you of the traumatic event

Avoidance

Symptoms of avoidance may include:

- Trying to avoid thinking or talking about the traumatic event
- Avoiding places, activities or people that remind you of the traumatic event

Negative changes in thinking and mood

Symptoms of negative changes in thinking and mood may include:

- Negative thoughts about yourself, other people or the world
- Hopelessness about the future
- Memory problems, including not remembering important aspects of the traumatic event
- Difficulty maintaining close relationships
- Feeling detached from family and friends
- Lack of interest in activities you once enjoyed
- Difficulty experiencing positive emotions
- Feeling emotionally numb
- Changes in physical and emotional reactions

Symptoms of changes in physical and emotional reactions (also called arousal symptoms) may include:

- Being easily startled or frightened

- Always being on guard for danger
- Self-destructive behavior, such as drinking too much or driving too fast
- Trouble sleeping
- Trouble concentrating
- Irritability, angry outbursts or aggressive behavior
- Overwhelming guilt or shame

For children 6 years old and younger, signs and symptoms may also include:

- Re-enacting the traumatic event or aspects of the traumatic event through play
- Frightening dreams that may or may not include aspects of the traumatic event

Intensity of symptoms

PTSD symptoms can vary in intensity over time. You may have more PTSD symptoms when you're stressed in general, or when you come across reminders of what you went through.

When to see a doctor

If you have disturbing thoughts and feelings about a traumatic event for more than a month, if they're severe, or if you feel you're having trouble getting your life back under control, talk to your doctor or a mental health professional. Getting treatment as soon as possible can help prevent PTSD symptoms from getting worse.

If you have suicidal thoughts

If you or someone you know has suicidal thoughts, get help right away through one or more of these resources:

- Reach out to a close friend or loved one.
- Contact a minister, a spiritual leader or someone in your faith community.

- Call a suicide hotline number — in the United States, call the National Suicide Prevention Lifeline at 1-800-273-TALK (1-800-273-8255) to reach a trained counselor.

We Don't Always Understand What We See

It is easy to pass judgment on the outward behaviors of people we observe. We may find those behaviors to be in poor taste or outright rude. We may be witnessing people presenting symptoms of PSTD and mistake it for lack of courtesy or assume a lack of respect for authority. Anyone who has not faced trauma, even the trauma (to some people) of a bad encounter with the police, is not prepared to properly relate to such persons.

I am a believer in taking personal responsibility, it is something we teach and model. However, as a pastor for 40 years I learned this important truth long ago: "There are always more broken hearts than hard hearts." The effects of a broken heart, wounded psyche, or personal violation, has effects on people that cannot be predicted. Many people and people groups have shared experiences. Most African-Americans have experienced injustice and disrespect. Fortunately, many of us were prepared by our parents to face such circumstances. Many of us learned not to overreact to a racist or insensitive comment. Many of us know the importance of doing exceptional work, sometimes more than is necessary, just to overcome the stigma the Black people do poor quality work.

As a professional digital media designer, I sometimes send my work ahead of me. In other words, I make sure persons see my work before they see my face. To some, this might seem excessively sensitive and defensive. My response would be, "Some of us have a different understanding of America than others."

The reality is, I am one of the highly rational Black people who knows how to process uncertainty and insults. Some African-Americans don't know how to do the same. Some people have been traumatized by their experiences and have either collapsed under the weight of it or have become bitter. Again, there's no excuse for irresponsible behavior, but one should not add insult to injury by showing callousness and dismissiveness towards people we don't understand.

Returning to the discussion about incarceration, especially related to overly harsh sentences, many people leave prison mentally and emotionally incapable of functioning effectively, without help and intervention. The term "institutionalization" is used to describe the process by which inmates are shaped and transformed by the institutional environments in which they live. Sometimes called "prisonization" when it occurs in correctional settings, it is the shorthand expression for the negative psychological effects of imprisonment.

> Changes in law and policy, not changes in crime rates, explain most of this increase. The trends include increasingly harsh policies and conditions of confinement as well as the much discussed de-emphasis on rehabilitation as a goal of incarceration. As a result, the ordinary adaptive process of institutionalization or "prisonization" has become extraordinarily prolonged and intense. Among other things, these recent changes in prison life mean that prisoners in general (and some prisoners in particular) face more difficult and problematic transitions as they return to the free-world.[71]

Into these complex problems we bring Christ. We don't come only to talk about Jesus and say prayers. We also come to help people connect with the wisdom of God and the presence of God. This is social justice expressed through our understanding of Biblical justice. Through wisdom, we connect willing people with resources and expertise to help them rebuild their lives. Most of all, we bring compassion, because people know when we are judging them and when we are help-

---

[71] *The Psychological Impact of Incarceration: Implications for Post-Prison Adjustment.* (2017). ASPE. https://aspe.hhs.gov/basic-report/psychological-impact-incarceration-implications-post-prison-adjustment

ing them. Even broken people maintain a sense of personal dignity that we must respect to gain access to their hearts and minds.

For persons returning to society from prison, there is the issue of recidivism, which is the instance of persons failing to adjust to post-incarceration and re-offending. In 2019 violent offenders recidivated at a rate of 63.8 percent compared to non-violent offenders who recidivated at a rate of 39.8 percent. [72] This is an area where prison ministry, a function of Biblical justice and social justice, has demonstrated a profound impact in reducing the rate of recidivism. An organization based in Indianapolis, Jesus Inside Prison Ministry, operates a residential re-entry program called, Jesus House. Men who complete parole through the program demonstrate a remarkable recidivism rate of 9-10%, or stated in the words of the Founding Director, Pastor William Bumphus, *"We have a success rate of 90%."* Details about their program are discussed in Chapter 15.

[72] *World Among Federal Violent Offenders.* (2019). United States Sentencing Commission. https://www.ussc.gov/sites/default/files/pdf/research-and-publications/research-publications/2019/20190124*Recidivism*Violence.pdf

Reflection Questions

1. Why are Black people incarcerated at higher rates?

2. What explains the higher rates of arrest and conviction?

3. How does Post Traumatic Stress Disorder (PTSD) affect people who've had bad encounters with the police or tragic incidents in their lives?

4. What is prisonization?

5. Why is recidivism a significant issue in our day?

6. What is the most effective methodology to reduce the rate of recidivism?

7. What Scriptural and social justice action can we employ to help with issues raised in this chapter?

CHAPTER 10

~

Blessings of Education and Perils of Mis-Education

Much of what we need to learn has been hidden or buried in the past. What we have learned has come from settings, schools, media, and persons to which we have been exposed. The objective of education is to prepare people, from childhood to adulthood, to live their lives and fulfill their purpose. Understanding the role of history and justice is a function of education.

Dr. Carter G. Woodson (1875 – 1950) was an author, editor, publisher, historian, and educator. Woodson earned a Ph.D. in history from Harvard University in 1912. He was a profound thinker whose concepts are relevant to this day. He is known as the "Father of Black History." He authored over 100 articles and more than 17 books, including the landmark work, *The Mis-Education of the Negro*. Woodson observed;

> These things must be viewed in their historical setting. The conditions of today have been determined by what has taken place in the past, and in a careful study of this history we may see more clearly the great theatre of events in which the Negro has played a part.[73]

We think of education as three R sounding words, "Reading, wRiting, and aRithmetic." These are important core competencies, but edu-

---

[73] Woodson, Cater G. (1933) *The Mis-Education of the Negro* (p. 15). (Public Domain). Kindle Edition.

cation is much more. In my State, the Indiana Department of Education developed the following standard in 2011: "Core 40 is the academic foundation all students need to succeed in college, apprenticeship programs, military training and the workforce we have adopted learning expectation expressed as Core 40, comprised of the following priorities."[74]

40 Credits Total

English/Language Arts - 8 Credits: Including a Balance of Literature, Composition and Speech.

Mathematics - 6 Credits

Science - 6 Credits

Social Studies - 6 Credits

Directed Electives - 5 Credits

Physical Education - 2 Credits

Health and Wellness - 1 Credit

Electives - 6 Credits

These are reasonable expectations for general education. Greater expectations of education will include components of learning and development, which may occur inside and outside the classroom. Of these *Core 40* requirements, the items that may impact character development and understanding of self include: **Language Arts and Social Studies.**

Since the time public schools became legally integrated, in places where segregation was once imposed, education has taken on more of a "one size fits all" approach. Some districts, such as suburban, where families are often homogenous, education should address the realities of a diverse population. Private schools, such as Christian, Jewish, Lutheran, Catholic and others, not only educate to academic standards, but also to socio-ethnic realities. The history of Black people in America

---

74   *Core 40 General Information | IDOE.* (2011). Indiana Department of Education. https://www.doe.in.gov/school-improvement/student-assistance/core-40-general-information

is distinct in ways that deserve historical attention. Black history is in part, the core of American history. Ugly truths like slavery, including the ownership of slaves by 25 of the 55 Framers of the Constitution, contradict assertions that the United States was founded as a Christian nation. Education should be about truth, not another platform to aggrandize religious or political narratives.

Mis-education has occurred in relation to Black history. This was the case at the Christian school that educated our four children. We underestimated the powerful forces of social and political conformity, apart from academics. We allowed ourselves and our children to become part of a cultural "gated community" that did not reflect our values and heritage as African Americans. They learned that Black people had been slaves, but they did not learn that false Christians and white supremacists were responsible for slavery. We wrongly believed public schools were inherently harmful, something we knew to be untrue because my wife has been an inner-city public school educator for 37 years. When we were young, we thought Christian school would "protect" our children from evil influences. In reality, children in some Christian schools are often walled off from the "real world" where Christ is also omnipresent and protecting His own. All of our children are successful professional adults today, because of the training we provided, college education, and the grace of God. Christian elementary and high school were not determinative factors to their success. They would have been successful at any good school, like their parents, grandparents, and great grandparents.

Mis-education in relation to Black history, which is a major component of American history, whether coming from willful neglect or disinterest, has a deleterious effect on the education of all children as becoming socially well-formed, beyond academics. Excluding the history of Black people in America not only creates a vacuum in learning but also in identity. Given the myths and lies about Black people, permitting the vacuum of a lack of Black history only attracts more of the worst perceptions and false narratives about Black people, as well as allowing white supremacy to go unchallenged. A lack of learning, which is a form of mis-education, includes how Black children perceive themselves.

The most imperative and crucial element in Woodson's concept of mis-education hinged on the education system's failure to present authentic Negro History in schools and the bitter knowledge that there was a scarcity of literature available for such a purpose, because most history books gave little or no space to the black man's presence in America.[75]

The Imperative of Black history Inclusion in School Curriculum

Curriculum is the philosophical basis of instruction in any school. Decisions about curriculum are among the most important decisions made by a school board, committees, and parents. Most curriculum has some elements of Black history. In 2005, Dr. Kenneth Sullivan, as the research topic of his doctoral dissertation conducted a qualitative research project on the Abeka curriculum, which is used by many Christian schools. The research found the following (Based on findings in 2005):

This study suggests that within the contemporary framework America still has a problem that needs to be examined and addressed. The research strongly suggests that the exclusion of people of African descent from the school curriculum has traditionally been a common practice in America. The research also suggests that inclusion of information about minorities will likely have a positive effect not only upon those being included but upon the broader student population as well (Brink 1963). Since Christians have the responsibility of modeling justice and fairness before the world, Christians should lead the way in addressing this void in the

---

[75] Wesley, C. (1969). *The Mis-Education of the Negro* - Introduction by Charles H. Wesley. History Is A Weapon. https://www.historyisaweapon.com/defcon1/ misedne.html

school curriculum from which America's children are taught (Ming 1993).[76]

This was a conclusion from 2005. Abeka may have improved Black history inclusion since that time. A thorough and positive presentation of African-Americans within school curriculum would serve to offset faulty perceptions and foster better race relations. This may be one of the greatest needs among private schools where curriculum selection may be more suited to the predominant culture. The Christian school that educated our four children did not offer a thorough approach to Black history.

As a white school, my wife and I accepted that lack of priority. In our interactions and meetings with the parent association and school administration, we made recommendations for greater Black history inclusion. Those recommendations went unheeded. Attention was given to world missions, which perhaps satisfied the school's diversity requirement. Part of the function of education in America, especially at a Christian school, should be preparing students to appreciate other cultures as well as learning to redemptively and intelligently relate to others. Students should also become better equipped to serve in settings different from their own.

"We must help people understand how the Bible addresses key questions concerning dignity, identity, and significance. Graduates who have this base of knowledge will be well equipped to serve the Lord in practical ways in urban ministry. The skewing of Biblical history that omits the contributions of people of color has a direct impact on the students who attend Christian schools. In many cases, Black students who attend evangelical schools come out less equipped to minister to Black people than when they went in!"[77]

---

76 Sullivan, Kenneth. *Abeka and Inclusion: An Analysis of the Degree to Which the Abeka Curriculum Includes the Contributions of People of African Descent.* (2005). Trinity College of the Bible and Theological Seminary. http://visioncomsolution-scom.siteprotect.net/Abeka*Curriculum*Sullivan*Dissertation.pdf*

77 Mason, Eric. *Woke Church* (pp. 149-150). Moody Publishers. Kindle Edition.

This would necessitate teaching Black history not only from the perspective of enslavement, but of the causes of slavery owing to white supremacy and false Christian doctrine. More importantly, a thorough presentation can offset the narratives of past brutality against Black people and present-day disrespect, by placing focus on the successes of African Americans throughout United States history. Christian education has a particular challenge as it relates to Black history because of the promulgation of inaccurate history and errant Bible doctrine.

Mis-Education in Christian School Curriculum

Below are some excerpts from Christian history textbooks posted by an independent writer: (**Note from Author:** These excerpts may have been updated by the publishers, but these represent examples of erroneous perspectives, whenever published, based on an intentionally biased presentation of history.)[78]

A few slave owners were undeniably cruel. Examples of slaves beaten to death were not common, neither were they unknown. The majority of slaveholders treated their slaves well. — **United States History for Christian Schools, A Beka Book**

Although the slaves faced great difficulties, many found faith in Christ and learned to look to God for strength. By 1860, most slaveholders provided Christian instruction on their plantations. — **America: Land I Love, A Beka Book**

To help His children endure the difficulties of slavery, God gave the Christian slaves the ability to spiritually combine the African heritage of song with the dignity and power of Christian praise. Through the Negro spiritual, the slaves developed the patience to wait on the Lord and discovered that the truest freedom is freedom from the bondage of sin. — **America: Land I Love, A Beka Book**

---

[78] Greczyn, A. (2020). *Christianity's Role in American Racism: An Uncomfortable Look at the Present and the Past*. Alice Greczyn. https://www.alicegreczyn.com/blog/christianitys-role-in-american-racism

The story of slavery in America is an excellent example of the far-reaching consequences of sin. The sin, in this case, was greed—greed on the part of African tribal leaders, on the part of slave traders, and on the part of slave owners, all of whom allowed their love for profit to outweigh their love for their fellow man. The consequences of such greed and racism extended across society and far into the future. It resulted in untold suffering—most obviously for the black race but for the white race as well. — **United States History for Christian Schools, Bob Jones University Press**

While these curricula seek to put slavery in a good light (with a few "bad" exceptions), the fact of "Christian" ownership of people was an affront to Christ and the New Testament Scriptures. References to "slaves" in the NT are related more to indentured servants. Holy Scripture cannot be used to justify the American form of slavery that featured rape, separating families, denial of inalienable rights. Moreover, is the fact that "Christians" bought and sold people with the blessing of the church. Believers in every generation should be guided the Scriptures,

All Scripture is given by inspiration of God, and is profitable for doctrine, for reproof, for correction, for instruction in righteousness, that the man of God may be complete, thoroughly equipped for every good work. (2 Timothy 3:16-17)

Following is a Scripture that was likely ignored by slaveowners, "Christian" and non-Christian:

"He who kidnaps a man and sells him, or if he is found in his hand, shall surely be put to death." (Exodus 21:16)

True Christians, like John Wesley, knew the truth about the sin of slavery and the necessity of its condemnation. (See Chapter 12, *"In the Words of John Wesley"*)

Educational Gated Communities

There are models of education, that are not cultural gated communities. The private Christian school my children attended required a signed statement of faith on the part of my wife and myself. They only wanted "Christians" at the Christian school. Again, at the time we thought this was the ideal state. In hindsight, we now know this educational structure was not a reflection of Biblical justice or social justice, howbeit well-meaning. During that time, there were other types of private Christian schools. We were aware of parochial or Catholic schools. They were less restrictive about the admission of non-Catholic students, but they held to beliefs and standards, as one would expect.

Urban Christian Schools

A friend and colleague founded an urban Christian school. At that time, there were no public charter schools and there were no taxpayer funded tuition vouchers for parents to send their children to a school of their choice. This Christian Academy was an extension of a successful preschool operated by him and his wife. The school offered first through sixth grades and an opportunity for preschool students to continue their education on a foundation of strong academics and Christ-centered values. There was the inclusion of Black history along with Black role models in the faculty and staff. The school was also connected to a church to provide spiritual uplift and discipleship.

The feature that distinguished this Christian school from the school my children attended was a philosophy that extended enrollment to all, Christian or non-Christian. There was no concern about non-Christians "spoiling" the Christian environment. On the contrary, as a work of social justice within Biblical justice, the founder and his team were confident that their love along with the power of Christ would become more influential on the children, and their parents, than any non-Christian influence one might bring. There was also a clear discipline policy and a no-nonsense approach to maintaining order within a productive learning environment. It was the type of school that an African-American could lead to educate African-American children as well as other ethnic groups. It was our hope that this Christian Academy (along with other preschools, such as ours) could become a model for African-American led, Christ-centered urban schools.

Economically, the school was supported by tuition as well as grants from charitable organizations and revenue support from their preschool operations. For younger children, parents could take advantage of State funding designated to help children of parents living below the poverty line. It was a great challenge to fund the school. There was the expectation that tuition vouchers would be beneficial to parents who wanted their children educated and nurtured in a private Christian school like this urban Christian school. However, these were the days before tuition vouchers were available. The founder, myself and a group of pastors formed a coalition to advocate on behalf of African Americans who operated or had a vision to operate, urban schools. Part of our work was to lobby our State legislature to adopt tuition vouchers in support of the school choice movement of that era. We thought school choice would greatly benefit urban people and Black enterprise in our city.

We were unsuccessful in gaining support for tuition vouchers. The state legislature decided to go with public charter schools. This was a great disappointment as we had worked with other organizations to achieve our goals. In the end, other partners achieved their objectives of getting the legislature and Governor to enact charter school legislation. Ironically and sadly, the adoption of tuition-free public charter schools undermined my friend's Christian school. Essentially, "free" was of more practical value than "Christian." A movement we helped to start and grow ended up cutting us out. The urban Christian school closed but the preschool operation has continued to thrive with Black role models, strong academics, and Christ-centered pre-education of young lives.

As an ironic end to this story, after establishing charter schools, our State finally approved tuition vouchers. However, they were not solely designated to serve the children of "poor" families as originally intended. The "universal" tuition vouchers provide tuition support for all families, including suburban families who can now send their children to private Catholic and Christian schools--including the school our children attended (They had to end their "Christian-only" policy to accept public money). A former governor of our state attended the ground-breaking of a multi-million dollar Christian school facility that was part of a mega-church outside of Indianapolis. Certainly, the adoption of universal vouchers helped to make it possible to build and fund this school.

The circumstances and outcomes of this story are not widely known. It was another evidence of how justice favors the privileged.

Self Determination is a Virtue

It was not a bad thing to be in partnership. We should have been more strategic as it relates to achieving our objectives. Carter G. Woodson wrote,

> History shows that it does not matter who is in power or what revolutionary forces take over the government, those who have not learned to do for themselves and have to depend solely on others never obtain any more rights or privileges in the end than they had in the beginning." [79]

A healthy outlook and self-image is well served by allowing children to learn about significant persons within their ethnicity and of others. Part of the purpose of teaching history is to help students round out their understanding of which people and what forces brought them to their present reality. History is full of triumphs and tragedies, heroes and villains, setbacks and breakthroughs, and most importantly seminal moments in history that brought dramatic change. One example is the landing at Plymouth Rock, the traditional site of disembarkation of William Bradford and the Mayflower Pilgrims who founded Plymouth Colony in December 1620. This event has its significance to our nation,

---

[79] Woodson, Cater G. (1933) *The Mis-Education of the Negro* (p. 116). (Public Domain). Kindle Edition.

but telling Black history brings sobering and needed perspectives to all such stories.

For example,

> As John Rolfe noted in a letter in 1619, "20 and odd negroes" were brought by a Dutch ship to the nascent British colonies, arriving at what is now Fort Hampton, then Point Comfort, in Virginia. Though enslaved Africans had been part of Portuguese, Spanish, French and British history across the Americas since the 16th century, the captives who landed in Virginia were probably the first slaves to arrive into what would become the United States 150 years later. [80]

These details do not diminish traditional stories that we learn about American history. In fact, history is enriched by truth and facts. Also, in the 21st-century, we need to reverse the trends that hid the plight of early Black Americans and minimized the impact of white supremacists' attitudes and practices. We know that there were white Europeans who were enslaved as indentured servants. However, the prospect of capturing and using strong Africans as a free labor force completely changed the economic paradigm for the colonies and for the early United States. Christian theology was crafted to justify the treatment of Africans as less than human as creatures fit only for the tasks of servitude and toil.

Rather than look at history through the Whites-only perspective of some 20th Century history writers, we should examine unbiased history from ethnically diverse 21st-century sources and writers. We should use those enlightened eyes to view history and maintain an appropriate outrage to the mistreatment of people made in the image of God. A proper telling of history should not bury the ugly truths of the mistreatment of Native Americans and Africans. Truth will not diminish the celebration of American history.

---

[80] Shah, K. (2019). *400 years since slavery: a timeline of American history*. The Guardian. https://www.theguardian.com/news/2019/aug/15/400-years-since-slavery-timeline

Overcoming Black History Mis-education

If a race has no history, if it has no worthwhile tradition, it becomes a negligible factor in the thought of the world, and it stands in danger of being exterminated. (Woodson, 1933)

Black History should begin with a basic timeline of events related to Africans and African Americans. Timelines consist of items which may not be comprehensive, but it is a good place to start. The Wikipedia Timeline of African-American history is informative. Follow the footnote at the end of this sentence. Because Wikipedia entries may be the edited by the public, it is important to follow links to primary sources.[81]

The Guardian publication published a concise and graphic-rich presentation of a slavery timeline from 1620 to 1965.

Follow the footnote to see the entire presentation. Below is a summary from the Guardian.[82]

1619

After the first captives were forced on to Virginia's shores by a Dutchman in 1619, the majority of the country remained white and relied mainly on the labor of Native American slaves and white European indentured servants. It was not until the end of the 17th century that the transatlantic slave trade made its impact on the American colonies.

1661

The first anti-miscegenation statute – prohibiting marriage between races – was written into law in Maryland in 1661, shortly after enslaved people were brought to the colonies. By the 1960s, 21 states, most of them in the south, still had those laws in place.

---

[81] Wikipedia Contributors. (2020). *Timeline of African-American history* - Wikipedia. Wikipedia. https://en.wikipedia.org/wiki/Timeline_of_African-American_history

[82] Shah, K. (2019). *400 years since slavery: a timeline of American history.* The Guardian. https://www.theguardian.com/news/2019/aug/15/400-years-since-slavery-timeline

Alabama was the last state to repeal the ban on interracial marriage in 2000.

1776

The Declaration of Independence, which embraced in its first lines "that all men are created equal, that they are endowed by their creator with certain unalienable rights", did not extend that right to slaves, Africans or African Americans, with the final version scrapping a reference to the denunciation of slavery. Thomas Jefferson, a slaveowner himself, penned those lines rejecting slavery; he removed the reference after receiving criticism from a number of delegates who enslaved black people. This could represent "the fabric of the American political economy," some historians have said.

Slavery flourished initially in the tobacco fields of Virginia, Maryland and North Carolina. In the tobacco-producing areas of those states, slaves constituted more than 50% of the population by 1776. Slavery then spread to the rice plantations further south. In South Carolina, African Americans remained a majority into the 20th century, according to census data.

1860

The British-operated slave trade across the Atlantic was one of the biggest businesses of the 18th century. Approximately 600,000 of 10 million African slaves made their way into the American colonies before the slave trade – not slavery – was banned by Congress in 1808. By 1860, though, the US recorded nearly 4 million enslaved black people – 13% of the population – in the country as the American-born population grew. Eight of the first 12 US presidents were slave owners. Proponents of slavery supported the efforts of groups like the American Colonization Society, who "sent back" tens of thousands of free black people – most of them American-born – to Liberia in the 19th century to prevent disruption caused by free descendants of slaves.

1865

According to Abraham Lincoln, the civil war was fought to keep America whole, and not for the abolition of slavery – at least initially. Southern states said they wanted to secede to protect states' rights, but they were really fighting to keep people enslaved. Lincoln took on the fight for the freedom of slaves, some historians have suggested, because he was worried the British would support the south in its self-declared self-determination and recognize the south as a separate entity. If he had made the war about ending slavery, it would have looked bad for the south's fight and the British supporting its cause. Lincoln's death was probably the first casualty of "a long civil rights movement that is not yet over," the historian Peter Kolchin has suggested.

1868

Some experts have argued that Reconstruction laid the foundation for "the organization of new segregated institutions, white supremacist ideologies, legal rationalizations, extra-legal violence and everyday racial terror" – further widening the racial divide among blacks and whites. Others have pointed out that the end of the war left black Americans free but their status "undetermined", with the passing of "codes" to prevent black people from being truly free.

But eventually, under the 14th amendment, African American men were granted the right to vote. Also, African Americans were extended birthright citizenship: that extends to descendants of freed black slaves and immigrants to present day.

1898

The recession of the late 19th century hit the US. Knight Riders went out in the dark, burning the homes of African Americans who bought their own land. They rode up to Washington to demand change as southern white Democrats rolled back many of the albeit limited freedoms from Reconstruction just a couple of decades before. The Jim Crow era of segregation forbade African Americans from drinking from the same water fountains, eating at the same restaurants or attending the same schools as white Americans – all lasting until, and sometimes well past, the 1960s.

1926

As African Americans were shut out of jobs and opportunities during Jim Crow, and as more jobs became available in the north and midwest, more than 2 million southern African Americans migrated after the first world war. Still, even hundreds of miles away from southern segregation, these migrating Americans were met by "sundown towns", where black people were not welcome after sunset, and by restrictions on where they could live in cities. Oregon's constitution, for example, only removed its exclusionary clause, prohibiting black people from entering the state, in 1926.

1954

In the lead-up to the end of Jim Crow and the civil rights era, the fight continued. For example, only in 1948 did the US military desegregate, by executive order. In 1954, in the Brown v Board of Education ruling, the supreme court ruled that segregation was unconstitutional and schools would have to integrate. Civil rights leaders led anti-segregation marches across the country in the 1960s. In 1964, President Lyndon Johnson signed the Civil Rights Act into law. Bussing African American children to white schools in white neighborhoods was deemed constitutional.

1965

"Slavery was gone but Jim Crow was alive. Almost all southern African Americans were shut out of the ballot box and the political power it could yield," wrote Edward E. Baptist in The Half Has Never Been Told: Slavery and the Making of American Capitalism. The Voting Rights Act of 1965 attempted to correct this, prohibiting racial discrimination in voting and placing restrictions on a number of southern states if they tried to change voting rights laws. Those restrictions were recently overturned in a 2013 supreme court ruling.

We need to overcome the false narratives about our national history and tell the unvarnished truth. The type of integrity we display as people today is impacted by the integrity with which we handle our history. White Americans comprise the majority of our population and have been in control of the narratives about our history. As the nation becomes more diverse, we must change our approach to education to become more inclusive. We no longer have an excuse to mis-educate, and the citizenry has the means to hold educators accountable. Despite all of the spurious and false claims of history, it is possible to get out the truth. This should be the goal of education.

Reflection Questions

1. What is mis-education?

2. What are some examples of mis-education?

3. What are the special challenges of Christian and home schools related to teaching Black history?

4. What are some inaccurate or poorly worded statements from some Christian school curriculum related to Black history?

5. What are 3-5 nation changing events from our history?

6. How can race relations benefit from teaching a more accurate version of Black History in Christian and home schools?

7. What Scriptural and social justice action can we employ to help with issues raised in this chapter?

CHAPTER 11

~

Race Relations, Ten Suggestions

About six-in-ten Americans (58%) say race relations in the U.S. are generally bad, a view that is held by majorities across racial and ethnic groups. Still, blacks (71%) are considerably more likely than whites (56%) and Hispanics (60%) to express negative views about the state of race relations.[83]

For the whole of my adult life "race relations" have been news items, but it has not been an item of discussion in my day-to-day life. As the poll data suggests, Black people tend to feel worse about "race relations" given the circumstances we have faced. White people are largely oblivious to the effects of racism against Black people, so they report that it is less of a problem.

As an African American, I don't recall ever having a conversation specifically about race relations with another Black person. We've talked about problems in our Black communities, bad encounters with White folks, white supremacy, police brutality, and inequities in housing, finance, education, and a number of other areas of concern. "Race relations" seems to be one of those issues, like ozone depletion, that is part of the news, but not part of daily life.

---

[83] *How Americans see the state of race relations.* (2020). Pew Research Center. https://www.pewsocialtrends.org/2019/04/09/how-americans-see-the-state-of-race-relations/

The Pew Research poll on race relations is more a measure of one's feelings than an actual measure of how people treat one another. There is no single authority on race relations. It seems the best we can do is listen to one another and learn--which is a good thing. The subject of race, and Black-White racial concerns in particular, come into focus and debate in the United States mainly in the news, on social media, and in designed meetings on the topic of race.

Consistent with the theme of this book, I will offer my perspectives on the topic of race. As stated in the introduction, the following are the thoughts of one man.

Indignant, Dismissive, or Utopian?

People seem to feel either indignation or become dismissive of racial concerns. For some, a sense of indignation grows from perceived or real slights and injustices which are too often racial in nature, to varying degrees. Those who are dismissive do not believe that race could be a significant factor in 21st century America and therefore conclude that race issues are manufactured or caused by the same people (Usually African Americans) who express grievance based on slights and injustices experienced. The following quotation capsulizes a dismissive posture from a position of ignorance:

"Of course, without question, racism against blacks has existed in America's past. And yes, it still exists today—but it's a lot harder to find." [84]

Still, others have a posture of trying to hover "above the fray" regarding all things racial and ethnic--displaying a kind of racial utopian worldview.

Whether one is Indignant, Dismissive, Utopian, or something else, race in America can never be ignored because racial factors are part of the fabric of our nation. Many of our national symbols carry the Latin

---

[84] Sullivan, N. B. (2020, February 18). *Five Ways Social Justice Stands in Opposition to Authentic*, Biblical Justice. Word Foundations. https://www.wordfoundations.com/2019/03/16/five-categories-of-contrast-social-vs-biblical-justice/

statement, *E Pluribus Unum,* meaning "Out of many, one." This national fabric was woven by the Framers and by the decisions and actions of early Americans. We have a strong constitutional foundation. Good and bad threads comprise our social fabric, and there is no denying history or the effects of history on every generation. What we need to do is continue to better ourselves. We need to weave new and better fabric, in order to change "future" history.

Of the three states: Indignant, Dismissive, and Utopian, history has proved that indignation is the most useful catalyst to social change. (On a different level, spiritual awakening and revival bring moral change to the heart).

Indignation has served to bring about change and create new standards of justice. Including the Declaration of Independence in 1776, anti-slavery abolitionists, the Underground Railroad, woman's suffrage (voting rights) movement, civil rights movement in Dr. King's day, 911 inspired counter-terrorism, national reactions to mass shootings and bombings, and the killing of George Floyd as representative of the abuse of Black men by bad cops. Indignation can provide a starting point for positive change in a pluralistic society. In the end, what must prevail is civil debate, clear thinking, better laws, just treatment, Godly influences, and a willingness to work together to find solutions. Unfortunately, dismissive and utopian attitudes are not helpful to the process of change/justice. It is antithetical to our American concept of social progress. It is better to "mix it up" so long as we do not become rude and intransigent. This was the concept behind Martin Luther King's concept of "direct action."

There are believers who will insist that our whole nation and government should be run based on the Holy Scriptures, but this is another utopian idea called Christian nationalism. It is impractical in a sinful world and nation where people cannot be compelled to obey the Bible. Biblical government and civil government are not the same. The Framers understood this principle, which is why there is no mention of Scripture in the Constitution. The Kingdom of God is spiritual in nature and is expressed through the lives, actions, and witness of followers of the Lord Jesus Christ. If we had "Biblical" civil government, all non-Christian religions could be deemed illegal. Some Christians might declare the practices of other Christians as "illegal." However, as "salt and light" Christians in the USA have, and should continue to have, the greatest influence on our nation, so long as our own sins don't undermine our moral authority. (2 Chronicles 7:14)

10 Suggestions for Relating to Black People & Overcoming Black Stereotypes

As an African American, I can best comment from the perspective of a Black man in our society. The suggestions that follow represent personal insights and a measured expression of indignation:

1. Do not lecture persons or offer commentary on an entire ethnic/racial group to which you neither belong nor deeply serve. (Romans 14:4)

2. Avoid the pretense of understanding people you do not know. Economic status and social "class" are not reliable indicators of a person's character and lifestyle.

3. Do not assume that the actions of one or some members of an ethnic/racial group indicate anything significant about that whole group of people.

4. Neither believe nor promote the lie that Black people operate under any kind of "curse." Note: Noah's "curse" was pronounced on Canaan not Ham (Gen. 9:25), whose descendants long ago died off. Most importantly, Genesis 9:1, states, *"God blessed Noah and his sons..."* Ham was blessed by God and could not be cursed, not even by (a drunken) Noah.

5. Do not highlight and share negative statistics about Black people while overlooking the overwhelming, and under-reported, amount of good, godly deeds and heroic contributions of African American persons. There's more to talk about than

Black crime (which has actually declined in the past ten years, but will always be unacceptable). "Non-Black" crimes such as insider trading and mass murder are no less unacceptable. We must focus on improving ourselves and helping others around us! No one is "color blind."

6. We should avoid rendering people's lives and circumstances as "invisible," but recognize, celebrate, and engage with people who are different from yourself.

7. Acknowledge that there is one "race"-- which is the "human" race, which is comprised of many ethnicities and nationalities. (Revelation 7:9). The whole concept of race, or people as "species," is a divisive concept. There is no such thing as "black blood" or "white blood."

8. Celebrate difference, uniqueness, and seek unity within diversity, not conformity through uniformity.

9. Hold persons accountable who exhibit behaviors of racial superiority, paternalism, or engage in stereotypical portrayals of individuals who should rather be viewed as made in the image and likeness of God.

10. Keep your heart and mind clear of presumption, judgment, hatred, xenophobia (fear/loathing of "other" people) and qualify your love for God by how you love people. (1 John 4:20)

Reflection Questions

1. Why do Black people and White people have a different understanding of the state of what we call "race relations?"

2. How many races of people exist today?

3. What 2-3 items from the list of suggestions speak to you?

4. What Scriptural and social justice action can we employ to help with issues raised in this chapter?

CHAPTER 12

~

In the Words of John Wesley, "Thoughts On Slavery"

This chapter will feature an excerpt from a pamphlet published by John Wesley in 1774, *"Thoughts Upon Slavery."* From our perspective, it was an anti-slavery article written in the spirit of justice with a view towards social justice on behalf of enslaved people. It was also a commentary on the culture of Africans and their communities from first hand accounts. He argued against justifications that were used to deceive and enslave Africans. Wesley also showed how slavery greed and profit motivations of some Europeans corrupted Africans and communities which they encountered.

Revisionist history has sought to keep the founding of America as a "Christian nation" in the best light. Wesley exposed lies behind justifications for slavery, such as "rescuing" Africans from a worse life in their native land. In this day, John Wesley experienced the "Good Trouble" of standing against injustice and doing social justice spoken about by the late John Lewis.[85] While Methodists became complicit in American Slavery, the Englishman and Preacher John Wesley was decidedly abolitionist in philosophy.

One the most effective ways to refute false narratives and revisionist history is to study accounts and perspectives of people who lived in

---

[85] Ray, R. (2020). Five things John Lewis taught us about getting in "good trouble." Brookings Institution. https://www.brookings.edu/blog/how-we-rise/2020/07/23/five-things-john-lewis-taught-us-about-getting-in-good-trouble/

an era. These words by the great preacher and Christ Follower, John Wesley, have been obscured by romanticized versions of American History.

From The Abolition Project:[86]

About John Wesley (1703-1791): John Wesley was an early leader in the Methodist movement in England. Under his direction, Methodists became leaders in many areas of social justice, including prison reform and the abolition of the Slave Trade. In 1736-7, Wesley visited North America including Georgia, which was then a British colony, and there he came into contact with enslaved people. This experience left him with a loathing of slavery but at first he felt unable to act on this. From 1739 onwards, Wesley and the Methodists were persecuted by clergymen and magistrates. They were attacked in sermons and in print and at times attacked by mobs.

The focus that Wesley needed came when Granville Sharp contested the case of a runaway slave (James Somerset) in the courts. Wesley was moved to study a text by the Philadelphia Quaker, Anthony Benezet. Wesley's journal shows that Benezet's work, and Lord Mansfield's deliberations in the case of Somerset, caused him much disquiet.

Two years later, in 1774, he wrote a tract called "Thoughts on Slavery" that went into four editions in two years. In it, he attacked the Slave Trade and the slave-trader with considerable passion and proposed a boycott of slave-produced sugar and rum. In August 1787, he wrote to the Abolition Committee to express his support. In 1788, when the abolition campaign was at its height, he preached a sermon in Bristol, one of the foremost slave trading ports. In those days, an anti-slavery sermon could not be preached without considerable personal risk to the preacher and a disturbance broke out.

He maintained an interest in the abolition movement until he died. Wesley also famously said: *"Give liberty to whom liberty is due, that is,*

---

[86]   John Wesley (1703-1791): *The Methodist Minister:* (2020). The Abolition of Slavery Project. http://abolition.e2bn.org/people32.html

to every child of man, to every partaker of human nature. Let none serve you but by his own act and deed, by his own voluntary action. Away with all whips, all chains, all compulsion. Be gentle toward all men; and see that you invariably do with every one as you would he should do unto you."

"Thoughts Upon Slavery" By John Wesley 1773[87]

Author Note: The lengthy excerpt that follows was written by the Englishman John Wesley. Some of the words are from the English language and spelling of his day. Follow the footnote to read his entire article.

GENESIS, Chap. IV, *"And the Lord said--What hast thou done? The voice of thy brother's blood crieth unto me from the ground".*

By slavery I mean domestic slavery, or that of a servant to a master. A late ingenious writer well observes, "The variety of forms in which slavery appears, makes it almost impossible to convey a just notion of it, by way of definition. There are however certain properties which have accompanied slavery in most places, whereby it is easily distinguished from that mild domestic service which obtains in our own country.

Slavery imports an obligation of perpetual service, an obligation which only the consent of the master can dissolve. Neither in some countries can the master himself dissolve it without the consent of judges appointed by law. It generally gives the master an arbitrary power of any correction not affecting life or limb.--Sometimes even these are exposed to his will: or protected only by a fine, or some slight punishment, too insiconderable to restrain a master of an harsh temper. It creates an incapacity of acquiring anything, except for the master's benefit. It allows the master to alienate the slave, in the same manner as his cows and horses. Lastly, it descends in its full extent from parent to child, even to the latest generation.

---

87   Wesley, J. (1778). *Thoughts upon Slavery. John Wesley,* 1703-1791. https://docsouth.unc.edu/church/wesley/wesley.html

The beginning of this may be dated from the remotest period, of which we have an account in history. It commenced in the barbarous state of society, and in process of time spread into all nations. It prevailed particularly among the Jews, the Greeks, the Romans, and the antient Germans: And was transmitted by them, to the various kingdoms and states, which arose out of the ruins of the Roman empire. But after christianity prevailed, it gradually fell into decline in almost all parts of Europe. This great change began in Spain, about the end of the eighth century: And was become general in most other kingdoms of Europe, before the middle of the fourteenth.

From this time slavery was nearly extinct, till the commencement of the fifteenth century, when the discovery of America, and of the western and eastern coasts of Africa, gave occasion to the revival of it. It took its rise from the Portuguese, who to supply the Spaniards with men, to cultivate their new possessions in America, procured negroes from Africa, whom they sold for slaves to the American Spaniards. This began in the year 1508, when they imported the first negroes into Hispaniola. In 1540 Charles the fifth, then king of Spain, determined to put an end to negro-slavery: Giving positive orders, That all the negro slaves in the Spanish dominions should be set free. And this was accordingly done by Lagasea, whom he sent and impowered to free them all, on condition of continuing to labour for their masters. But soon after Lagasea returned to Spain, slavery returned and flourished as before. Afterwards other nations, as they acquired possessions in America, followed the examples of the Spaniards; and slavery has now taken deep root in most of our American colonies.

Such is the nature of slavery: Such the beginning of negro-slavery in America. But some may desire to know, what kind of country it is, from which the negroes are brought? What sort of men, of what temper and behaviour are they in their own country? And in what manner they are generally procured, carried to, and treated in America

Africa Before the Slave Trade

And first, What kind of country is that from whence they are brought? Is it so remarkably horrid, dreary and barren, that it is a kindness to deliver them out of it? I believe many have apprehended so: But it is an entire mistake, if we may give credit to those who have lived many years therein, and could have no motive to misrepresent it.

That part of Africa whence the negroes are brought, commonly known by the name of Guinea, extends along the the coast, in the whole, between three and four thousand miles. From the river Senegal, (seventeen degrees north of the line) to Cape Sierra Leona, it contains seven hundred miles. Thence it runs eastward about fifteen hundred miles, including the Grain-Coast, the Ivory-Coast, the Gold-Coast, and the Slave-Coast, with the large kingdom of Benin. From thence it runs southward, about twelve hundred miles, and Concerning the first, the Senegal-Coast, Mons. Brue, who lived there sixteen years, after describing its fruitfulness near the sea, says, "The farther you go from the sea, the more fruitful and well-improved is the country, abounding in pulse, Indian corn, and various fruits. Here are vast meadows, which feed large herds of great and small cattle. And the villages which lie thick, shew the country is well peopled." And again: "I was surprized, to see the land so well cultivated; scarce a spot lay un-improved: The low lands divided by small canals, were all sowed with rice: The higher grounds were planted with Indian corn, and peas of different sorts. Their beef is excellent; poultry plenty and very cheap, as are all the necessaries of life."

As to the Grain and Ivory Coast, we learn from eye witnesses, that the soil is in general fertile, producing abundance of rice and roots. Indigo and cotton thrive without cultivation.--Fish is in great plenty; the flocks and herds are numerous, and the trees loaded with fruit.

The Gold-Coast and Slave-Coast, all who have seen it agree, is exceeding fruitful and pleasant, producing vast quantities of rice and other grain, plenty of fruit and roots, palm-wine, and oil, and fish in great abundance, with much tame and wild cattle. The very same account is given us of the soil and produce of the kingdoms of Benin, Congo and Angola--From all which it appears, That Guinea in general, far from being an horrid, dreary, barren country, is one of the most fruitful, as well as the most pleasant countries in the known world. It is said indeed to be unhealthy. And so it is to strangers, but perfectly healthy to the native inhabitants.

Such is the country from which the negroes are brought. We come next to enquire, What sort of men they are, of what temper and behaviour, not in our plantations, but in their native country. And here likewise the surest way is to take our account from eye and ear witnesses. Now those who have lived in the Senegal country observe, it is inhabited by three nations, the Jaloss, Fulis, and Mandingos. The king of the Jaloss has under him several ministers, who assist in the exercise of justice. The chief justice goes in circuit through all his dominions, to hear complaints and determine controversies. And the viceroy goes with him, to inspect the behaviour of the Alkadi, or Governor of each village. The Fulis are a numerous people; the soil of their country represented as rich, affording large harvests, and the people laborious and good farmers: Of some of these Fuli blacks who dwelt on the river Gambia,

William Moor the English factor gives a very   account.--He says, they are governed by their chief men, who rule with much moderation. Few of them will drink any thing stronger than water, being strict Mahometans. The government is easy, because the people are of a good and quiet disposition; and so well instructed in what is right, that a man who wrongs another is the abomination of all.-- They desire no more land than they use, which they cultivate with great care and industry: If any of them are known to be made slaves by the white men they all join to redeem them. They not only support all that are old, or blind, or lame among themselves; but have frequently supplied the necessities of the Mandingos, when they were distrest by famine.

The Mandingos, says Mons. Brue, are rigid Mahometans, drinking neither wine nor brandy. They are industrious and laborious, keeping their ground well cultivated, and breeding a good flock of cattle. Every town has a governor, and he appoints the labour of the people. The men work the ground designed for corn; the women and girls, the rice-ground.--He afterwards divides the corn and rice among them: And decides all quarrels if any arise. All the Mahometan negroes constantly go to public prayers thrice a day: there being a priest in every village, who regularly calls them together: Some authors say it is surprizing to see the attention and reverence which they observe during their worship.--These three nations practise several trades; they have smiths, sadlers, potters and weavers. And they are very ingenious at their several occupations.--Their smiths not only make all the instruments of iron, which they have occasion to use, but likewise work many things neatly in gold and silver. It is chiefly the women and children who weave fine cotton cloth, which they dye blue and black.

It was of these parts of Guinea, that Mons. Adanson, correspondent of the royal academy of sciences at Paris from 1749 to 1753, gives the following account, both as to the country and people. "Which way soever I turned my eyes, I beheld a perfect image of pure nature: An agreeable solitude, bounded on every side by a charming landscape; the rural situation of cottages, in the midst of trees; the ease and quietness of the negroes, reclined under the shade of the spreading foliage, with the simplicity of their dress and manners: The whole revived in my mind the idea of our first parents, and I seemed to contemplate the world in its primitive state. They are generally-speaking, very good-natured, sociable and obliging. I was not a little pleased with my very first reception, and it fully convinced me, that there ought to be a considerable abatement made, in the accounts we have of the savage character of the Africans." He adds, "It is amazing that an illiterate people should reason so pertinently concerning the heavenly bodies. There is no doubt, but that with proper instruments, they would become excellent astronomers."

The inhabitants of the Grain and Ivory-Coast are represented by those that deal with them, as sensible, courteous, and the fairest traders on the coasts of Guinea. They rarely drink to excess: If any do, they are severely punished by the king's order. They are seldom troubled with war: If a difference happen between two nations, they commony end the dispute amicably. The inhabitants of the Gold and Slave-Coast likewise, when they are not artfully incensed against each other, live in great union and friendship, being generally well-tempered, civil, tractable, and ready to help any that need it. In particular, the natives of the kingdom of Whidah are civil, kind, and obliging to strangers.--And they are the most gentleman-like of all the negroes, abounding in good manners towards each other. The inferiors pay great respect to their superiors:--So wives to their husbands, children to their parents. And they are remarkably industrious: All are constantly employ'd; the men in agriculture, the women in spinning and weaving cotton.

The Gold and Slave-Coasts are divided into several districts, some governed by kings, others by the principal men, who take care each of their own town or village, and prevent or appease tumults.-- They punish murder and adultery severely; very frequently with death.--Theft and robbery are punished by a fine proportionable to the goods that were taken. All the natives of this coast, though heathens, believe there is one GOD, the author of them and all things. They appear likewise to have a confused apprehension of a future state. And accordingly every town and village has a place of public worship.--It is remarkable that they have no beggars among them:

Such is the care of the chief men, in every city and village, to provide some easy labour, even for the old and weak. Some are employ'd in blowing the smiths bellows; others in pressing palm-oil; others in grinding of colours. If they are too weak even for this, they sell provisions in the market.

African Culture Not Barbaric

The accounts we have of the natives of the kingdom of Benin is, that they are a reasonable and good-natured people, sincere and inoffensive, and do no injustice either to one another or to strangers.--They are civil and courteous: If you make them a present, they endeavour to repay it double. And if they are trusted, till the ship returns next year, they are sure honestly to pay the whole debt.--Theft is punished among them, although not with the same severity as murder. If a man and woman of any quality, are taken in adultery, they are certain to be put to death, and their bodies thrown on a dunghill, and left a prey to wild beasts. They are punctually just and honest in their dealings; and are also very charitable: The king and the great lords taking care to employ all that are capable of any work. And those that are utterly helpless they keep for GOD'S sake; so that here also are no beggars.

The inhabitants of Congo and Angola are generally a quiet people. They discover a good understanding, and behave in a friendly manner to strangers, being of a mild temper and an affable carriage.--Upon the whole therefore the negroes who inhabit the coast of Africa, from the river Senegal to the southern bounds of Angola, are so far from being the stupid, senseless, brutish, lazy barbarians, the fierce, cruel, perfidious savages they have been described, that on the contrary, they are represented by them who had no motive to flatter them, as remarkably sensible, considering the few advantages they have for improving their understanding:--As very industrious, perhaps more so than any other natives of so warm a climate.--As fair, just and honest in their dealings, unless where whitemen have taught them to be otherwise:--And as far more mild, friendly and kind to strangers, than any of our forefathers were. Our forefathers! Where shall we find at this day, among the fair-faced natives of Europe, a nation generally practicing the justice, mercy, and truth, which are related of these poor black Africans? Suppose the preceding accounts are true, (which I see no reason or pretence to doubt of) and we may leave England and France, to seek genuine honesty in Benin, Congo, or Angola.

We have now seen, what kind of country it is, from which the negroes are brought: And what sort of men (even whitemen being the judges) they were in their own country. Enquire we, Thirdly, In what manner are they generally procured, carried to, and treated in America.

First. In what manner are they procured? Part of them by fraud. Captains of ships from time to time, have invited negroes to come on board, and then carried them away. But far more have been procured by force. The christians landing upon their coasts, seized as many as they found, men, women and children, and transported them to America. It was about 1551, that the English began trading to Guinea: At first, for gold and elephants teeth, but soon after, for men. In 1566, Sir John Hawkins sailed with two ships to Cape Verd, where he sent eighty men on shore to catch negroes. But the natives flying, they fell farther down, and there set the men on shore, "to burn their towns and take the inhabitants." But they met with such resistance, that they had seven men killed, and took but ten negroes. So they went still farther down, till having taken enough, they proceeded to the West-Indies, and sold them.

Corruption of African People

Here it may be well to give a particular account of that transaction in the very words in which it is transmitted to us by early historians, as it is a clear proof, that it was solely from a desire of gain that the English first undertook to seize and bring the unhappy Africans from their native country; and is a clear and positive refutation of those false arguments frequently advanced in vindication of the slave trade, viz. That the first purchase of negro slaves by the English, was from motives of compassion, with views of saving the lives of some of those blacks who being taken prisoners in battle, would, if not thus purchased, have been sacrificed to the revenge of their conquerors: but this plea is manifestly false; from all the accounts we have of the disposition of the negroes in those early times, they appear to have been an innocent people, gentle and easy in their nature, rather averse to war, as is the general disposition of the natives of these warm climates; till being corrupted by an intercourse with the Europeans, and stimulated by the excessive use of spirituous liquors, they were induced to join them in their cruel depradations against their unhappy countrymen. The account given of that transaction by Thomas Lediard in his naval history, at page 141, is in the following words:

"That Sir John Hawkins in his several voyages to the Canary Islands, understanding that negroes were a very good commodity in Hispaniola, (then settling by the Spaniards) and that they were easy to be had in great numbers on the coast of Guinea. Having opened his mind to his friends, he soon found adventurers for his undertaking; amongst whom were Sir Lionel Docket, Sir Thomas Lodge, and others: and having fitted out three small vessels, manned only with 100 men, he departed from the coast of England in October 1562, and sailed first to Teneriffe, where he took in several refreshments; from thence to the coast of Guinea, where he got in possession, partly by the sword, and by other means, upwards of three hundred of the natives, besides several commodities which that country afforded: with this bootxsy he set sail for the island of Hispaniola in the West-Indies; where he disposed of his negroes. Two years after, he went another voyage on the coast of Guinea; there he staid several days at the island Sabula, where every day they took some of the inhabitants; burning and ravaging their towns: when having compleated their number of negroes, they set sail for the West-Indies."

Read the entire pamphlet by following the footnote.[88]

---

[88]   Wesley, J. (1778). *Thoughts upon Slavery. John Wesley,* 1703-1791. https://docsouth.unc.edu/church/wesley/wesley.html

Reflection Questions

1. What 3-5 points from John Wesley's pamphlet, "Thoughts On Slavery" stand out to you?

2. How could Wesley's perspectives and preaching have been overlooked and ignored in his day?

CHAPTER 13

~

The Myth Of The Monolith

"You degrade us, and ask me why we are degraded—you shut our mouths, and then ask why we don't speak—you close your colleges and seminaries against us, and then ask why we don't know more." (Frederick Douglass)

F ew things degrade the dignity of individuals more than questioning a person's willingness to make progress. It is equally insulting to assign the problems or perspectives of some, to the many. African Americans, more than any other group of people, seem to labor under the perception that they think alike, act alike, or lack individual objectivity.

The Power of Thinking

Black people do not help disprove the Black Monolithic myth by uncritically parroting the concepts and words of others. Our unity on essential matters will not be threatened by free thinking or by challenging the status quo in the interest of arriving at better solutions.

Certainly, we should continue to stand together on matters pertaining to justice and progress as a people, but remain free to dissent when necessary. Organizations such as the NAACP and the Urban League are necessary organizations to facilitate the coalescing of Black unity on particular issues.

It should be obvious that Black people do not think the same. Certainly, this book is evidence of that reality. Those who have a different perspective—which seeks to improve the condition of Black people and others—should not be criticized or ostracized because of thinking "out of the box." The media (both mass media and social media) sometimes plays to this Black monolithic narrative through the reporting and portrayals of Black concerns. Many African Americans for reasons of work and a lack of disposable time, don't have the opportunity to thoroughly read and research some of the key issues of our day. Like many Americans, there is the problem of "low information" that relies almost exclusively on superficial information sources such as television news, social media, or casual conversation. As a result, many people are mis-educated and misinformed on some issues. This is an area where leaders and organizations, including churches, can provide resources and accurate information.

Ways in which African Americans can challenge the monolithic myth:

1. By affirming that each of us is made in God's image and likeness.

2. By being well informed through reading and listening to thorough, reputable, and accurate materials

3. By engaging others on issues outside of the African American community to gain better perspectives and share insights

4. By seeking to establish a Black presence in institutions which have lacked such a presence.

Ways in which White people can challenge the monolithic myth:

1. By resisting any urge to judge Black people based on pre-conceived notions.

2. By listening carefully to arguments on issues of personal concern, without interjecting oneself. Consider responsible African Americans as "Subject Matter Experts" (SME)

3. By not regarding any one person as a spokesman for all African Americans.

4. By reading the works of Black intellectuals and Christian leaders and studying the works of persons from history such as Rev. Dr. Martin Luther King and Dr. Carter G. Woodson.

Ultimately, any monolithic perception degrades full appreciation of the individual. Pre-judging or being dismissive of persons destroys one's own potential for growth because of missing out on contributions due to a lack of attentiveness.

Jesus said, "Do not judge according to appearance, but judge with righteous judgment." (John 7:24)

As a "minority" group of 44 million people, African Americans must stand together to maintain moral and political clout. As citizens, we need unity in order to command the attention of policy makers. As Christ Followers, we need to live Scriptural principles of righteousness (and justice), as well as practice social justice by how we live and serve others.

Reflection Questions

1. How does the Myth of the Monolith hinder Black people?

2. How does the Myth of the Monolith hinder White people?

3. How do we overcome it?

4. What Scriptural and social justice action can we employ to help with issues raised in this chapter?

CHAPTER 14

~

What Can We Do?

"Not everything that is faced can be changed. But nothing can be changed until it is faced." ~James Baldwin

Questions surrounding what we can do to bring about so-called "racial reconciliation" or heal the divide between the races is common in our culture. We need to ask better questions. One better question might be, "Should racial reconciliation be our objective? Is something more fundamental needed?"

This last point is only beginning to dawn on us white Christian Americans, who still believe too easily that racial reconciliation is the goal and that it may be achieved through a straightforward transaction: white confession in exchange for black forgiveness. But mostly this transactional concept is a strategy for making peace with the status quo—which is a very good deal indeed if you are white. (Robert P. Jones)[89]

Another good question might be "How does reconciliation relate to conciliation?" The quest for racial reconciliation often bypasses the more important need to address injustice. Conciliation, like mediation, is understood as a process of facilitating communication between the two parties having a dispute or difference. Conciliation is a process

---

[89] Jones, Robert P.. *White Too Long: The Legacy of White Supremacy in American Christianity* (p. 235). Simon & Schuster. Kindle Edition.

that, like a fruit tree, only bears fruit over time with care and cultivating.

In our Christian culture, we are keen on holding events as if the event makes a difference and brings change according to the title of the event. Robert P. Jones, in his book *White Too Long*, a scholar and person raised within Southern Baptist Convention churches, addressed the SBC reckoning with its past of supporting slavery and racial bigotry in the 19th and 20th Centuries. Jones observed that the acknowledgment of past sins and injustices on the part of the SBC did not result in significant structural change going forward. Jones noted that actions were limited to "lament and apology."

> In his 2015 article, Mohler [Then SBC president] declared, "We must repent and seek to confront and remove every strain of racial superiority that remains." Yet in the cover letter to the report, he distances himself from current action required by this past with the following theological flourish: "We must repent of our own sins, we cannot repent for the dead." One foot forward, shuffle back. (Robert P. Jones)[90]

This statement on behalf of the Southern Baptist Convention is correct on its face, but did not go far enough to change the culture of SBC. The school had named buildings after founders who were slave-owners, which represented heresy and error. Repeated calls to rename buildings have been rejected.

> *Again, the sole action of lament and apology preserves the sense of satisfaction and does not disturb the consciousness of church and convention members. It was John the Baptist who said "bring forth fruit meet for repentance." (Matthew 3:8)*

The breath and depth of white supremacy is rarely appreciated and often relegated to the past or understood as isolated occurrences in the

---

Jones, Robert P.. *White Too Long: The Legacy of White Supremacy in American Christianity* (p. 16). Simon & Schuster. Kindle Edition.

present. White supremacists are often viewed only as the extremist, KKK, cross-burning types. Robert P. Jones writes:

> If we slow down enough to reexamine the plain meaning of the phrase, its continued relevance comes clearly into view. Even rearranging the words—from "white supremacy" to "supremacy of whites"—gets us closer to a clearer meaning: the continued prevalence of the idea that white people are superior to, or more valuable than, black and other nonwhite people. [91]

This is the mindset that needs to be addressed, not in the context of feeling guilty, but within the reality of inertia within white culture. Examining the issue another way, white supremacy (or attempted supremacy by anyone) is a massive failure of the mandate to love.

Living in Love is the Key

Within any relationship, there are challenges. Especially with those who we love enough to speak frankly and even confront. Scripture makes the case that we should even love people we don't know. God loved each of us to the level of sacrifice that He sent Jesus to suffer and die for us, for the purpose of lifting us up out of our sinful selves. We don't have to die for one another, but there may be some suffering as we sacrifice to lift up one another. A lot of the problems that we face would be easier to solve if we prioritized walking in love. In his book, *The Woke Church,* Dr. Mason writes,

> Our division in the church in America is rooted in disconnection from one another. And that, my Christian brothers and sisters, should not be.[92]...Family loves on one another. Family takes care of one another. Family is patient with one another.[93]

---

[91] Jones, Robert P.. *White Too Long: The Legacy of White Supremacy in American Christianity* (p. 16). Simon & Schuster. Kindle Edition.

[92] Mason, Eric. Woke Church (p. 24). Moody Publishers. Kindle Edition.

[93] Ibid. p. 59

Dr. Mason suggests several action items to heal relationships and restore the church back to an effective witness. One of those items is accountability:

> Be accountable. Where there has been silence in the past, we now have the awesome opportunity to reclaim our roles as light and salt in our world. We need to be known for speaking the truth to one another in love so that we can deal effectively with the problems of race and injustice in the church and in the world. In doing so, we become an effective gospel community with a ferocious prophetic voice. The call to be a Woke Church requires us to reclaim our Biblical identity as the people of God. (Eric Mason) [94]

Accountability Within Our Relationships

Accountability among our family, friends, and even among strangers can be an effective tool. *"As iron sharpens iron, so one person sharpens another." Prov. 27:17*

A cable news network hosted a panel discussion about racism in America[95]. One of the significant points of action that was suggested highlighted an instance at a Philadelphia Starbucks in which two African-American men experienced bad treatment by an employee who called the police to report them as "trespassing." The police handcuffed and arrested them. A viral video shows a White customer defending the young men in front of the police officers[96], the employees, and other customers. It was a spontaneous example of how one person can come to the aid of another. In this instance, a White gentleman showing concern for fellow Black citizens. Two young Black "wrongdoers" (not an uncommon perception) were supported by a "stranger" who acted as a concerned fellow citizen. He sought to hold the Starbucks employee

---

[94] Ibid p. 34

[95] *America's racial reckoning must happen, leaders say at MSNBC town hall.* (2018). NBC News. https://www.nbcnews.com/news/nbcblk/msnbc-s-everyday-racism-america-racial-reckoning-must-happen-leaders-n878336

[96] *Social media video shows arrests of black men at Philadelphia Starbucks.* Guardian News https://www.youtube.com/watch?v=xWBVxTEgoYk

and the police officers accountable for the wrongful apprehension of the young men. They were still arrested and taken away, but the viral video provided yet another example of injustice against Black men, with the twist of a White gentleman using his privilege in attempting to defend the honor and innocence of the Black men.

We all possess a certain level of privilege in which we are able to do something or be perceived in a way that other people cannot.

The Power of Privilege - My Story

We can use our privilege to address bigotry and racism. Privilege can be defined as a special right, advantage, or immunity granted or available only to a particular person or group. There is no absolute cure for bigotry and racism because sin and evil possess the hearts of people who are unwilling to change.

First of all, I am defining racism in a narrow sense as disrespect, bad treatment, and marginalization of African-Americans by persons who feel superior or entitled as a "ruling class." Certainly, racism by Black people towards White people exists, but it is small in effect and largely powerless since Black people do not control very much in the larger society. Black racism is more of a nuisance. Not as many White folks face problems being subject to Black people who hold power.

Racism in the form of whites against blacks (or other ethnic minorities) is far more harmful owing to majority status, holding more influential and impactful stations in life. Nearly every Black person has a White boss or works for a White employer. It is an inarguable fact that most reported acts of bigotry and racism in the USA have occurred against African-Americans. (Note: In many ways, Black people are representative of all other people of color).

There is a pervasive problem that makes people appear racist when they are not. When people who are not racist remain silent about their awareness of others within their circles who display racist behaviors or attitudes, they perpetuate the problem. We've all known people who have "crossed the line." We permit problems to persist when we don't speak up to address people we know.

SUGGESTED SOLUTION ONE

Help, educate, and correct your family, acquaintances, and friends

If anyone within my sphere of influence displays bigoted or racist behavior (and that would be mostly African-Americans), I will take the responsibility to address that matter, person to person. There are not many actions more impactful than being confronted by a friend.

It is likely that every racist person has a non-racist acquaintance or friend who has had the occasion to be appalled at something he has seen or heard from his friend, acquaintance, or family member. When we fail to take the opportunity to address people within our sphere of influence, we permit that behavior to go unchallenged, which may result in the spread of undesirable behaviors.

SUGGESTED SOLUTION TWO

Use Your Privilege

Three Stories:

We all have privilege in the sense that we carry a certain level of influence and authority that others might not carry. Without being actively aware, we have access to places and people that others do not have. It is not possible to be fully aware of one's privileges because we are living it and are unaware of any other standard.

Story #1

When I was 19 years old and in college, I made a big mistake following a concert that landed me in the lock-up at the downtown police headquarters. I spent the night in jail and was scheduled to appear in court the next morning. I was scared and nervous watching weekend "regulars" brought in to that large room. I saw the chaos, witnessed fights, and just prayed that I could sleep through it. With my one phone call, I called my father. Even though I did not serve God and disrespected Him, He showed me mercy and let me sleep through the chaos all night, unharmed, on a narrow metal bench against a wall.

The next morning they brought a number of us into a holding cell behind the courtroom for a judge to hear our charges. I knew my father would be out there to help me through the situation. However, when I appeared before the judge, my father was not in the room, and there was no one to represent me. The judge ordered that I be taken back to the holding cell. That was one of the most devastating feelings one could imagine.

As it turned out, my father went to the wrong courtroom. After some time passed, my name was called, and I came from the holding cell to the courtroom and saw my father standing with an attorney. This young African-American attorney happened to be in the court room when I came out the first time. Somehow, he connected with my father because he observed that I "seemed out of place" and saw my dad was distressed looking for me (perhaps the attorney identified with me in some way). He was not seeking a client, and my father was not looking for an attorney. This attorney used his privilege to help me. He didn't have to do it, but he did.

It is amazing what can be done when we use our privilege to help somebody in difficulty. What is more amazing is using our privilege to defend the dignity and honor of people being insulted or mistreated.

Story #2

Many years ago as a pastor our church had the occasion to purchase a commercial property on a prominent street to use as our main facility, We were denied a zoning variance for reasons that were unjust and racially motivated because of the nature of the opposition we faced. In a meeting to which I was "invited," I was handed a list of "suitable" inner-city properties and "encouraged" to pursue one of those instead of the one we wanted. When we refused, this group of businessmen influenced the zoning board to oppose us.

We retained an attorney and appealed to Superior Court. We easily won the day and overturned the zoning board's decision on Constitutional grounds when the city attorney decided to drop their case because he couldn't win. What made the difference, in addition to the expertise of my attorney, was that the seller of the property assigned his own attorney to join in the effort to help us (and of course, to help conclude his sale). The seller, a White gentleman, who happened to be a wealthy owner of a commercial real estate company, personally knew many of the business people who opposed us. The seller used his privilege and influence to help us.

Story #3

I read a story of two sisters who looked very different. The one looked more African-American and the other looked like a White lady. They were both shopping at the same grocery store. The sister who looked more like a White person was in line in front of her sister. The cashier rang up her items and she presented a personal check for payment (which was more the custom at that time).

When her African-American looking sister presented her check, the cashier reached for a binder in which the store kept copies of bad checks. The cashier proceeded to scan the names on the bad checks looking for a match. The cashier made the bigoted assumption that the Black looking lady might be trying to pass a bad check.

When her sister saw it, she returned to the checkout and asked the cashier what she was doing. In the presence of the cashier, her sister, and other White customers, she demanded that the cashier accept her check in the same manner the other lady's was accepted. No one could've known this was her sister.

It looked like a White person using her privilege to defend the honor of a Black person.

Again, 1) Help, educate, and correct your family, acquaintances, and friends, and 2), Use your privilege.

I remember a sad occasion on a Facebook friend's discussion thread. One of his Facebook friends publicly insulted and disparaged me, my church, and my family (in an indirect way) when I expressed a strong disagreement within the discussion. I privately asked him how he was going to handle it. He said he would write a personal note to the man. I advised him that friends stand up for friends in the same place where things happen, anywhere in life. He made the choice not to use his privilege to publicly stand up for me.

Each of us needs to take responsibility within our spheres of influence. We also need to rid ourselves of leaders who perpetuate bigotry and racism. We must not enable such persons through silence, inaction, or support. Persons demonstrating racist behavior need to be educated and reproved by people who know them. Legal action should be taken when laws are violated. We should not coddle bigots and racists.

If we lovingly and directly handle matters within our spheres of influence, I believe progress can be made.

> *Somehow, the best theological minds figured out how "love your neighbor" did NOT apply to the racism and injustice (and, by the way, I mean injustice the way the Bible defines injustice) that black people were experiencing, oftentimes at the hands of professed Christians, in both church and community.* (Dr. Eric Mason) [97]

---

[97] Mason, Eric. Woke Church (p. 16). Moody Publishers. Kindle Edition.

Reflection Questions

1. Why does seeking racial reconciliation alone fall short?

2. Why is "lament and apology" inadequate?

3. Why is accountability effective?

4. What is privilege? How do we benefit from it? How can we use privilege to benefit others?

5. Is there anyone within my circle of influence who has expressed racist or bigoted behavior that I need to address?

CHAPTER 15

~

Success Stories

There have been many sobering discussions over the course of this book. I am aware that there is a general fatigue as it relates to discussions about race, injustice, and unpleasant aspects about history. There are times when people who are engaged in difficult conversations drop out. It was not unlike the old arcade games that would stop working and display the word "TILT" if the machine was jarred or jostled by a frustrated gamer. People often reach a point at which one does not want to hear "any more bad news." The hard fact is this: One person's bad news is another person's daily reality.

As a pastor for four decades, I've lived on the edge of people's pain, joys, sorrows, sicknesses, death, and even anger and disrespect directed towards me. Pastors, like all first responders, have a high threshold of handling bad news. Everyone in the business of serving people, must practice self-care. We see that Jesus took his own disciples aside to rest and eat. (Mark 6:31) David, the Psalmist, spoke about being led beside "still waters" and causing the flock to lie down in "green pastures." (Psalms 23)

We've taken on some difficult topics and have taken a hard look at some important issues in contemporary life and from history. Challenges and struggles have a fruitful side. Because our labors are never in vain, we sometimes get to see good outcomes. Following are a few stories that reflect good outcomes of social justice and good works born out of Biblical justice, which is God's righteousness.

Jesus Inside Prison Ministry

There's no organization closer to the front lines of the good and bad outcomes of civil justice than a prison ministry. The success story of Jesus inside Prison Ministry is well worth sharing.[98] This ministry is one of the best examples of Biblical justice working within a Christ-centered organization, resulting in the effective outworking of righteousness in social justice.

In Chapter Eight, we talked about incarceration, emotional trauma, and disturbing statistics regarding crime and African-Americans. Our criminal justice system is overburdened with cases and many of our prisons are overcrowded. The United States leads the world in the number of persons incarcerated. We've already addressed concerns about mass incarceration and sentencing.

There is another very important phase within the area of Corrections. That important phase is called **re-entry**. What happens with men and women when they finish serving their time and come back out into the world? The hope is that people will leave prison, forsake a life of crime, and become productive persons and taxpayers. This is the hope, but unfortunately the reality is far different. In the field of Corrections there is a word called **recidivism**. It is the phenomenon of people who leave prison that end up re-offending, being re-arrested, and charged with another crime. There's also something called the **rate of recidivism** which is represented as a percentage. In 2019 violent offenders recidivated at a rate of 63.8 percent compared to non-violent offenders who recidivated at a rate of 39.8 percent. That is an alarming rate of human failure. [99]

One of the most remarkable stories in corrections is the work of Jesus Inside Prison Ministry and their aftercare facility called, Jesus

---

[98]   Jesus House. (2020). Jesus Inside Prison Ministry. https://www.jipm.org/jesus-house

[99]   *Recidivism Among Federal Violent Offenders.* (2019). United States Sentencing Commission. https://www.ussc.gov/sites/default/files/pdf/research-and-publications/research-publications/2019/20190124*Recidivism*Violence.pdf

House. This ministry was founded by a friend and colleague, Pastor William Bumphus 40 years ago from this writing. He turned to Christ while incarcerated and accepted a call to ministry. The success of the work can be objectively measured by one astounding metric. In a nation, where the rate of recidivism hovers between 45 and 70%, the Jesus Inside Prison Ministry aftercare program and facility called Jesus House has reduced the recidivism rate to 9 to 10% for men who complete their program.

In an interview with Pastor Bumphus, we discussed the causes of the high rate of recidivism. Two primary factors were cited: 1) A lack of safe housing for men leaving prison. Returning to the same neighborhood often becomes a trap, since it represents a return to the same environment that contributed to criminal behavior. 2) An unprepared mindset and lifestyle. Prison is a controlled environment in which inmates do not make many decisions for themselves. They are told when to wake, sleep, eat, work, go to the restroom, or go outdoors for recreation. Months and years of living in a controlled environment disables the ability to make quality decisions. Of course, some persons never developed good decision making, which contributed to ending up in prison.

Pastor Bumphus also explained that incarceration is not about reformation and rebuilding lives. It is about warehousing people for as long as their prison sentence has dictated. Making any improvement comes from the initiative of the prisoner himself. Most prisons have education programs such as GED which is a high school equivalent diploma. There are other programs in some prisons of which inmates may take advantage. Pastor Bumphus and his team have visited over 560 prisons in the USA and Africa. The ministry has distributed hundreds of thousands of Gospel books. He has eight books in print.

As measured by the success of reducing recidivism, the most effective program for reforming men released from prison is the model used by the Jesus inside Prison Ministry. Pastor Bumphus calls their methodology, "*A strong discipleship program.*" The objective is to help men complete their two year parole—which they call, "getting off paper." As communicated by Pastor Bumphus, the specific features of their Jesus House discipleship program include:

1. Before release from prison, inmates must request an application to the Jesus House from the prison Chaplain. They do not accept men with backgrounds of sex crimes.

2. Inmates must indicate on the form that they are believers in Jesus Christ. Whether their confession is genuine or not, Pastor Bumphus states that their predisposition towards faith in Christ is an important first step. Everyone learns that the facility is 100% Christian. As a privately funded program, they are free to mandate Biblical principles.

3. When "Returning Citizens" (the term they used rather than ex-offenders) are released from prison, they must come straight to the Jesus House to become a resident.

4. Residents don't need to bring anything with them. Everything is provided including lodging, food, and clothing. This reduces concerns about needs and allows residents to focus on the program

5. Attendance to Bible study is required twice every weekday. Prayer is taught and practiced daily. Sunday church attendance is mandatory. The philosophy is that men lived within a negative controlled environment in prison. Jesus House is also a positive controlled environment. Daily Bible study is necessary to help men change their mindsets through the Biblical process of "renewing the mind." *And do not be conformed to this world, but be transformed by the renewing of your mind, that you may prove what is that good and acceptable and perfect will of God.* (Romans 12:2) Also during this time, if men entered Jesus House without a genuine conversion to Christ, the opportunity is presented during the discipleship period. As an authentic Biblical ministry, the truths of the

Word of God become real in the lives of men. One key Scripture is 2 Corinthians 5:17 that reads, *"Therefore, if anyone is in Christ, he is a new creation; old things have passed away; behold, all things have become new."* Another key scripture for discipleship is: *"But seek first the kingdom of God and His righteousness, and all these things shall be added to you."* (Matthew 6:33)

6. Work is not mandatory, but guys who get jobs are asked to pay a nominal amount for weekly rent. The work schedule cannot interfere with Bible Study to Sunday church services.

7. Random drugs tests (called "drops") are conducted by "Resident Directors," who are men (usually former residents) who live at Jesus House to provide leadership and administration.

8. In addition to Bible Study, other teaching takes place such as Biblical finance and personal development. Additionally, for guys who are ready, lessons on how to repair their credit and learn how to own real estate.

From my long experience with Jesus Inside Prison Ministry as a supporter, and a speaker from time to time, I have witnessed many changed lives. Hundreds of men have passed through the program. The vast majority have landed on their feet, becoming godly men, taxpayers, and productive citizens. Many have become business owners, excellent employees, leaders within other organizations, pastors, and more. Many men have been restored to their families. Others have become married and have started families. There have been some heartbreaking situations over the course of decades of service, but JIPM has been the best example effective ministry within a community.

Freetown Village

History has been described as "His Story." Freetown Village is a "living history" museum founded in 1982 based in Indianapolis.[100] The

---

[100] *Our Mission & History.* (2020). Freetown Village. https://www.freetown.org

mission is to educate the public about African American lives, arts, and culture in Indiana through living history, exhibits, allied programs, and the collection and preservation of artifacts. The Founding Director, Ophelia Wellington is an educator, historian, and story teller. Freetown Village portrays a fictional settlement (based on actual research) at Indianapolis in 1870. In the portrayals, faith in God was central to the community, consistent with narratives from that time. During the era called "Reconstruction" following the Civil War, Black people exercised their new freedoms and found their way forward. Given the evidence that Christianity was used to justify evils such as slavery and segregation, it is remarkable that African Americans managed to navigate around disingenuous religion to discover the genuine Christ. There is the mistaken view that Africans only discovered Christ when they were brought to America as slaves. As far back as the First Century, the African continent was touched by the message of the Gospel of Jesus as told in Acts 8:26-38.

Freetown Village has reached hundreds of thousands of people through performances before various audiences, through digital media, events, schools, and full stage plays. The Black history stories they portray show principles of Biblical justice through the faith of the people as well as their concerns about civil justice as recently emancipated former slaves. This was the era during which the 13th Amendment had been ratified, which did more than the Emancipation Proclamation of 1863. The Constitutional amendment brought freedom to four million people. While Black people initially flourished as federal troops protected newly freed Americans in southern states, the white backlash was swift and brutal after the death of Abraham Lincoln. Vice President Andrew Johnson became president, who put the interests of former slave over newly freed Black people.

Freetown Village performances puts a sharp focus on the progress and positive dynamics of African American life during 1870.

Tabernacle Presbyterian Church

(The information below is from the church website. www.tabpres.org)

In the heart of Indianapolis is a church that has exemplified the principles of Biblical justice and social justice for more than 169 years.

Tabernacle Presbyterian Church was founded on September 23, 1851.[101] The "tabernacle movement," an international movement led by Charles Spurgeon at Metropolitan Tabernacle in London, was a strategy to reach and welcome unchurched people in urban areas through a less formal approach to worship as a means to make church more accessible. The church moved to its current site at the corner of 34th and Central in 1921. In 1924, the Tab Recreation program was established to meet the recreational and athletic needs of the children in the church and community. Tab was one of the first churches in the country to establish a recreation program as part of its outreach and ministry.

In 1961, the church integrated its ministry and programs during a time of racial division, prior to civil rights legislation. In 1965 a decision was taken to stay at its current location and not move out to the suburbs as many other churches begin to do at that time. With full recognition of the changes in the neighborhood, increasing racial tension and violence, the migration of church members, as well as many other churches and businesses moving to the suburbs, Tabernacle Presbyterian Church made the decision to stay in order to be *"A force for Christ in the Heart of the City."*

In 2009 the church recommitted itself to continued ministry at its location by adopting a new mission statement:

Tabernacle Presbyterian Church is called by God, led by faith in Jesus Christ and empowered by the Holy Spirit to demonstrate the Kingdom of God through worship, discipleship and outreach. Honoring our heritage at 34th and Central, we will faithfully serve

---

101 Tab Story (2020). Tabernacle Presbyterian Church. www.tabpres.org/

our community, city and world in the present and prepare expectantly for the future.[102]

Tabernacle Presbyterian Church has always been committed to a "two-legged Gospel," a balance of evangelical witness from the pulpit and social involvement in the community. One without the other is insufficient in living out the whole Gospel. This was modeled in Jesus' ministry, in His preaching/teaching, as well as His healing/feeding, His care for the body as well as the soul.

In 1994 the church provided land and resources to establish an independent health center called Raphael Health Center.[103] The mission of Raphael (meaning "God Heals") was to provide a community centered, quality, affordable health care and related services in order to improve the health status of neighborhood residents and lessen sickness.

The word *"tabernacle"* means *"the dwelling place of God among His people."* Since 2007, Rev. L. John Gable has served as Senior Pastor.

Multimedia in Focus Media Camp

Since the year 2000, Multimedia In Focus, comprised of a team of mentors, digital artists, and myself have been inspiring and educating youth in the area of the media arts.[104] Having been educated in the media arts and instructional design (B.A. and M.S.) and working as a designer and producer for over 20 years (20 years ago), we recognized a void that needed to be filled. Reflecting on knowledge possessed today, we knew that media created a kind of injustice for young people. As a pastor and community leader (Th.B. and D.Min), we always look for ways to reach underserved populations and challenge any tide of injustice. We found that exposure to bad media influences, such as ex-

---

[102] Ibid.

[103] *About Raphael Health Center.* (2020). Raphael Health Center. https://raphaelhc.org

[104] *About Us.* (2017). Multimedia In Focus. https://www.visionmultimedia.org/index.html

treme violence or exploitation of women, caused negative effects. On the other hand, a void in understanding media and a lack of skills in using media created barriers for them. At that time we did not used the language of justice and injustice. We simply thought that something was "wrong" with the status quo.

The story of how we began to make a difference initiated with a conversation I had with a pastor friend. In that conversation, I complained about the negative effects of media on young people. At the time, I was leading a church, doing traditional youth ministry, and all the things that churches do. My professional media work was not something that was fully integrated into the church, even though we operated from the church and primarily served other churches as a non-profit service.

In the same moment that I complained to my friend about the negative impact of media on youth, it was as if the Lord said, *"What are you going to do about that?"* Looking back on that moment with today's understanding, I can see that the God of Justice was concerned about youth and the unrighteous, unjust, impact of media on them. During the same conversation, I told my pastor friend what had happened in my heart and mind. I committed to start a training program for youth, not knowing how we would do it. Not soon after that decision we became aware of a funding opportunity by Lilly Endowment, based in Indianapolis, called the Summer Youth Program Fund (SYPF). We put our vision to empower youth in writing for a media arts summer day camp. To my surprise, we received funding with our first application. In 2001, we held off first six week media camp called Multimedia In Focus. We had about 10 youth to participate. We struggled to find enough computers, cameras, other equipment, and skilled teaching staff, but in the end it came together!

From 2001 to 2017, with exception of one year, we held the Multimedia In Focus Summer Media and Arts Camp with funding provided each year. For many of those years through 2019, we also held weekend single day events called "Mini Camps." In addition to teaching youth how to do storytelling, produce videos, create various types of graphics—from 2D to animated 3D, and learn photography. We allowed our youth to use the same professional equipment that we used in our business. We reasoned that if we provided the best equipment and instruction, youth would give us the best work, and they did!

We invited media professionals to join us for "VisionTime" talks. Guests came from the fields of audio/video/animation production, recording engineers, news anchors from local television stations, reporters, photographers, visual artists, and educators from universities. We made trips to production houses and local universities allow young people to get a grasp on media degree programs. The training took place at our church and every day began with prayer. Again, looking back and applying today's understanding, we were doing **social justice** from the foundation of **Biblical justice**. Over the past 20 years, many of those young people have become working professionals in many fields including media arts, documentary producers, music, accounting, education, and other fruitful careers unrelated to media. They not only learned about media production, they learned about team building, personal organization, respect for authority, and gained appreciation that God provides the gifts that we are responsible to use for His glory.

We had "Crew Members" from all walks of life and from various religions and non-religion, including Islam. We served a large number of so-called "at risk" youth. In our program we never saw a young person as **"at risk,"** we viewed them as **"At Promise,"** in the words of Dr. Victor Rios, professor of sociology at University of California, Santa Barbara. Multimedia In Focus was our expression of social justice.

Reflection Questions

1. Why does practicing Biblical justice within our lives/churches produce social justice towards others?

2. What are some of my success stories?

3. What have I learned from social justices and righteous engagement with others?

4. Why is "at promise" better than "at risk?"

CHAPTER 16

~

Justice and Governing Authorities

This final chapter will feature a Bible study from Romans 13:1-7. Not many passages in the New Testament directly address civil government as it impacts all citizens, including those who self identify as Christians. This text does not address Biblical justice or social justice. It addresses the principle of civil justice. This study will focus on citizens of the United States. Let's first read the text,

> Let every soul be subject to the governing authorities. For there is no authority except from God, and the authorities that exist are appointed by God. 2 Therefore whoever resists the authority resists the ordinance of God, and those who resist will bring judgment on themselves. 3 For rulers are not a terror to good works, but to evil. Do you want to be unafraid of the authority? Do what is good, and you will have praise from the same. 4 For he is God's minister to you for good. But if you do evil, be afraid; for he does not bear the sword in vain; for he is God's minister, an avenger to execute wrath on him who practices evil. 5 Therefore you must be subject, not only because of wrath but also for conscience' sake. 6 For because of this you also pay taxes, for they are God's ministers attending continually to this very thing. 7 Render therefore to all their due: taxes to whom taxes are due, customs to whom customs, fear to whom fear, honor to whom honor. (Romans 13:1-7)

There are two key questions to address from the context of the country in which you are a citizen. For myself, that would be the United States:

1) What are the governing authorities?

2) Who is God's minister?

It is first important to understand context. One of the rules of Bible hermeneutics, or Bible interpretation, is to determine context. To whom did the apostle Paul write? What is the original, intended, plain meaning of this text? We must first begin with the fact that Paul wrote a letter in the First Century to Christians who were at Rome. These were people living under the government of the Roman Empire. The unelected emperor of Rome at the time of the Apostle Paul was Nero.

In Paul's day there was no government in the world anything like the United States of America, certainly not the Roman Empire. There was no government "of the people, by the people, for the people" as Abraham Lincoln said in his Gettysburg Address.[105] The Preamble of the United States Constitution reads:

> We the People of the United States, in Order to form a more perfect Union, establish Justice, insure domestic Tranquility, provide for the common defence, promote the general Welfare, and secure the Blessings of Liberty to ourselves and our Posterity, do ordain and establish this Constitution for the United States of America.

When Paul wrote, *"Let every soul be subject to the governing authorities. For there is no authority except from God, and the authorities that exist are appointed by God,"* we can understand the following:

1. Within our national context, *governing authorities* cannot be one person. No single president, senator, representative, governor, judge, or mayor represents governing authorities, because our form of government is pluralistic, as outlined in the Constitution by three co-equal branches of government: executive, legislative and judicial.

---

[105] Lincoln, A. (1863). *Gettysburg Address by Abraham Lincoln*. National Archives. https://www.archives.gov/historical-docs/todays-doc/?dod-date=1119

2. The United States was not designed to be a monarchy ruled by a king/queen or a dictatorship ruled by a dictator.

3. The United States is an exercise of self-government.

4. No person in the government of the United States is appointed by God. The people choose government leaders. Others in government may be appointed by people.

5. For United States citizens, the Biblical sense of "governing authorities" is the entire system of government at every level, federal, state, and local.

6. "For there is no authority except from God." "He is God's minister." This does not refer to a single person acting alone of his/her will apart from our Constitution and laws. The proper context is the "principle" of authority, which must be exercised according to laws and the United States Constitution.

7. Persons have authority, but no one is *the* authority.

8. The Bible does not grant any person in the United States special authority or power.

Romans 13:2-3 reads, *"Therefore whoever resists the authority resists the ordinance of God, and those who resist will bring judgment on themselves. For rulers are not a terror to good works, but to evil."*

This Scripture does not authorize law enforcement persons, such as police officers, who are not governing authorities, to shoot people who fail to comply or speak to them disrespectfully. They are certainly authorized by laws and rules of engagement (not by the Bible) to defend themselves and protect citizens.

In the United States we do not have "rulers" because we choose our political leaders. There is no lawful swift "judgment" in this country because our Constitution provides "Due Process."

Amendment XIV

Section 1.

All persons born or naturalized in the United States, and subject to the jurisdiction thereof, are citizens of the United States and of the state wherein they reside. No state shall make or enforce any law which shall abridge the privileges or immunities of citizens of the United States; nor shall any state deprive any person of life, liberty, or property, without due process of law; nor deny to any person within its jurisdiction the equal protection of the laws.

In fact, police officers do not qualify as governing authorities under our system of government. They are law enforcement officials, not "avengers" who "execute wrath" as described in Romans 13.

Former Attorney General Jeff Sessions erred in quoting the Bible to defend his President's policies in separating migrant children from their families at the U.S.- Mexico border.

I would cite you to the Apostle Paul and his clear and wise command in Romans 13, to obey the laws of the government because God has ordained them for the purpose of order," Sessions said, when defending President Trump's "zero tolerance" immigration policy.[106]

It was an overreach and self-serving to use Scripture to justify enforcement of a "law" that didn't exist, but worse to do so in support of his president's policy, not the will of Congress and the People. In reality, it is quite disingenuous for men to create a law and then say it is a law that God requires one to obey. This has occurred in our past where it was illegal for Black people to have lunch at a whites-only restaurant. The violation of which would have gone against "The ordinance of God" from Romans 13 in someone's view at that time

---

[106] Gobry, P. (2018). *What the Bible really says about government*. The Week. https://theweek.com/articles/779283/what-bible-really-says-about-government

In the United States we accept the responsibility to voluntarily obey laws. It is part of our self governing philosophy. We also choose to suffer consequences for disobeying laws.

Paul wrote, "For there is no authority except from God." He did not write this in support of the Roman Empire, but in support of the principle of "governing authority," which is necessary within society. In reality the Apostle Paul knew that people within the government of the Roman Empire were pagan and engaged in idolatry.

> In Rome, government wasn't just absolute, it was literally divine. "Roma" was a goddess; all public offices were also religious offices; and executions for high crimes were sacrifices to the gods.[107]

In our system of government and jurisprudence, magistrates, courts, constitutions, laws, statutes, and due process are our "authorities" "ministers" and "avengers." Paul wrote;

> *For rulers are not a terror to good works, but to evil. Do you want to be unafraid of the authority? Do what is good, and you will have praise from the same. For he is God's minister to you for good. (Romans 13:3-4)*

Again, individuals are not authorized by the Bible or by United States law to be "The Authority." We certainly respect all of our civil servants and government officials, but we know that some of them are not "a terror to evil" because some do evil themselves. Within our system, we have the means to remove such people. If their authority was solely from God, they could not be removed.

As stated in an earlier chapter, when Christians mis-apply the force of their religious convictions on civil government it creates confusion and a distortion of both the Christian faith and the role of government.

---

[107] Ibid.

For because of this you also pay taxes, for they are God's ministers attending continually to this very thing. 7 Render therefore to all their due: taxes to whom taxes are due, customs to whom customs, fear to whom fear, honor to whom honor. (Romans 13:6-7)

Citizens shared in the expense of government and the services of government to fellow citizens. We respect public servants because they are part of "governing authorities," and public servants respect the citizenry who made it possible for them to serve. Again, in America we have self-government and we are enjoined by God to submit to it. Submission may not always include obedience. For example, Rosa Parks disobeyed a "lawful" instruction to give up her seat at the front of the bus. However, she remained submitted to government and to God.

Reflection Questions

1. What are 1-2 of the biggest misconceptions about Romans 13?

2. What are the "governing authorities?"

3. How does the U.S. Constitution form of voluntary self-government fit within Romans 13?

4. How does "There is no authority except from God" fit within our system of elections, powers of impeachment, and man-made laws?

Conclusion

We have the opportunity to right the wrongs of the past. Not in reversing tragic deeds, but in correcting our understanding and telling of history. We need to acknowledge that the sin of subjugating fellow humans, who were made in the image and likeness of God was a great evil. Crafting false narratives to evade the truth of complicity by Christianity was another evil.

Failing to end slavery, but sowing into its expansion, at the founding of our nation, reaped a whirlwind of untold misery on generations that followed. The Civil War was chief among those horrors, followed by the backlash against newly emancipated Black Americans, during their strides of progress.

In this 21st-century, we don't need to escape from our past, we only need to own it, repent to God for the bad parts of it, and build new paths towards brighter days for our children.

When Christ Followers live by the principles of Biblical justice as served to our world through the righteousness of social justice, we will be able to give people the most valuable gifts we can offer, Jesus Christ and our love! As Peter said to the blind man who looked to him,

"Silver and gold I do not have, but what I do have I give you: In the name of Jesus Christ of Nazareth, rise up and walk."
(Acts 3:6)

Frequent Statements & Questions

(**Note:** Responses offered by the Author)

STATEMENT: I was raised to not see color. I am color blind.

RESPONSE: God is not color blind. We can celebrate the distinctiveness and diversity of humanity. The Apostle John shared a vision of heaven in Revelation 7:9-10, *After these things I looked, and behold, a great multitude which no one could number, of all nations, tribes, peoples, and tongues, standing before the throne and before the Lamb, clothed with white robes, with palm branches in their hands, and crying out with a loud voice, saying, "Salvation belongs to our God who sits on the throne, and to the Lamb!"*

STATEMENT: We should not have a Black History Month.

RESPONSE: Black History Month was established nearly a century ago by historian Carter G. Woodson for the reason that African-Americans were systematically whitewashed out of American history. Resistance to the concept of Black History Month (or anything Black) is evidence of systemic racism in our nation. A systemic problem presents itself in both diverse and subtle ways. Black History is American History and should be understood and taught because of the significant challenges and contributions of African Americans. Anyone who argues against recognizing Black History should argue against every ethnic and social recognition such as St. Patricks Day, Mardi Gras, Cinco De Mayo, Women's History Month, Autism Awareness Month, Oktoberfest, and dozens of others. America's diversity is its strength and is something to celebrate. Everyone is free to not recognize or celebrate any occasion.

STATEMENT: All the church needs to do is show Christian love and unity.

RESPONSE: The Bible provides specific guidance on how Christ Followers can positively impact people within our communities and beyond person-to-person. Jesus, His disciples, and believers in the Book of Acts modeled those actions. This book also addresses many of those Scriptural mandates and strategies.

STATEMENT: Social Justice is not Biblical Justice.

RESPONSE: The term "Social Justice" has been politicized like the term Black Lives Matter. However, just as "Black lives matter" is a statement of human concern and not only about the organization, social justice is related to doing Biblical righteousness (justice) within our community (social). We should focus on the character of people who serve, not on the political agendas of persons seeking to discredit the work of godly people by politicizing a term.

STATEMENT: Focusing on social unrest is negative and should be avoided by people of faith.

RESPONSE: Rev. Dr. King faced that criticism in his day. His actions and outcomes proved that he was on the right side of history. Our nation, and the church, are better for the work of Christian ministers and workers during that era. Social justice action is not for every believer and every church. The mission of the church is making disciples for Christ and preaching the Gospel. Our mission does not end with members of our churches or neglecting the physical needs of people who receive Christ as Savior. Again, this book addresses the work of Christ's church.

QUESTION: What is Manifest Destiny?

RESPONSE: Manifest Destiny, in U.S. history, the supposed inevitability of the continued territorial expansion of the boundaries of the United States westward to the Pacific and beyond. Before the American Civil War (1861–65), the idea of Manifest Destiny was used to validate continental acquisitions in the Oregon Country, Texas, New Mexico, and California. The purchase of Alaska after the Civil War briefly revived the concept of Manifest Destiny, but it most evidently became a renewed force in U.S. foreign policy in the 1890s, when the country went to war with Spain, annexed Hawaii, and laid plans for an isthmian canal across Central America. [108]

QUESTION: How can a Christian vote for a Democrat since they believe in abortion?

RESPONSE: Not all Democrats support abortion (while many do), just as not all Republicans support white supremacists (while many do). There is the lip service of saying "pro-life" while not actually engaging in actions that save unborn lives or help those who are born. Using the words "Pro-life" and speaking against all Democrats is a political tactic to drive votes for Republicans. It is the position of the Author that the most effective strategy today is to accept the responsibility to prevent abortion by teaching people to live right, counseling women to choose life, helping them and their children, when they choose life, holding men accountable, and supporting crisis pregnancy centers. If Roe v. Wade was overturned today, abortion would not become illegal nationwide. The matter would revert back to the states, as before 1973, where abortion was legal in some states and not in others. There is also the question of what to do with mothers who get abortions if it were illegal. Some Christians support the death penalty for such women and doctors.

QUESTION: What is the Seven Mountain mandates and is it Biblical?"

ANSWER: The Seven Mountains mandate or the Seven Mountains prophecy is an unBiblical movement that has gained a following in

---

[108] *Manifest Destiny*. (2020). Britannica Online. https://www.britannica.com/event/Manifest-Destiny)

some Charismatic and Pentecostal churches. Those who follow the Seven Mountains "mandate" believe that, in order for Christ to return to earth, the church must take control of the seven major spheres of influence in society for the glory of Christ including Education, Religion, Family, Business, Government-Military, Arts-Entertainment, and Media. Once the world has been made subject to the kingdom of God, Jesus will return and rule the world. It is interesting that health and medical are not included.[109]

PROVIDE YOUR FEEDBACK:

Visit the book website to offer your comments, questions, and suggestions. *www.biblicaljusticebook.com*

---

[109] *Got Questions* (2020). What is the seven mountain mandate, and is it biblical? Got Questions. https://www.gotquestions.org/seven-mountain-mandate.html

Glossary of Civil Justice

NOTE: *These limited definitions have been curated by the Author*

13th Amendment 1864 - The Constitutional Amendment that abolished slavery. As a compromise, the amendment does permit "involuntary servitude" (a form of slavery) as a form of "punishment" for incarcerated persons

14th Amendment 1868 - The Constitutional Amendment that guaranteed citizenship rights and equal protection of the laws to all (now including African Americans)**15th Amendment** - The Constitutional Amendment that prohibits the federal and state governments from denying a citizen the right to vote based on that citizen's race, color, or previous 1870 condition of servitude

ADA - Short for the Americans with Disabilities Act, the ADA protects persons with disabilities from discrimination in many aspects of life, including employment, education, and access to public accommodations

African American - An American of African and especially of black African descent. This ethnic designation became widely accepted because of its clear description of ethnic heritage. There is no place on the earth called Negro, or Colored. The term Black is also widely accepted.

Affirmative Action - Known as positive discrimination; policies that take factors including race, color, religion, sex, or national origin into consideration in order to benefit an underrepresented group

Antebellum - In the United States of America, of the period prior to the American Civil War, especially in reference to the culture of the southern states.

Black Power movement - The Black Power movement emerged during the Civil Rights movement in the late 1950s and early 1960s with the intention of promoting racial pride and black interests. The movement was not formally organized and had no central leader. The term black power was first used in the book Black Power, written by Richard Wright in 1959

Civil Rights The rights of individuals to be free from unfair or unequal treatment (discrimination) in a number of settings, when that negative treatment is based on the individual's race, gender, religion, national origin, disability, sexual orientation, age, or other protected characteristic.

Black Lives Matter (movement) A decentralized political and social movement advocating for non-violent civil disobedience in protest against incidents of police brutality and all racially motivated violence against black people.

Black Lives Matter (organization) Founded in 2013 in response to the acquittal of Trayvon Martin's murderer. Black Lives Matter Foundation, Inc is a global organization in the US, UK, and Canada, whose mission is to eradicate white supremacy and build local power to intervene in violence inflicted on Black communities by the state and vigilantes. By combating and countering acts of violence, creating space for Black imagination and innovation, and centering Black joy, we are winning immediate improvements in our lives. (wwwblacklivesmatter.com)

Black lives matter A statement of human concern about the bad treatment of Black people, unaffiliated with an organization or movement

Brown v. Board of Education of Topeka, Kansas. On May 17, 1954, the U.S. Supreme Court issued its unanimous ruling in the historic civil rights case Brown v. Board of Education of Topeka, Kansas. It held that school segregation violated the equal protection and due process clauses of the Fourteenth Amendment and was therefore unconstitutional. Almost sixty years earlier, the Supreme Court had ruled that separate but equal facilities were legal in Plessy v. Ferguson (1896), the precedent that Brown overturned. On May 31, 1955, the Court ordered the states to integrate public schools with all deliberate speed.

Civil Rights Act of 1964: A federal law that prohibits discrimination in a number of settings: Title I prohibits discrimination in voting; Title II: public accommodations; Title III: Public Facilities; Title IV: Public Education; Title VI: Federally-Assisted Programs; Title VII: Employment.

Conservative A political philosophy derived from the word conservative comes from conserve, hence describing those who generally wish to maintain the status quo, holding to traditional attitudes and values. Resistant to change typically in relation to politics and society.

Despot A ruler who has absolute power (or believes the same), especially when the ruler is cruel in his exercise of power.

Discrimination Discrimination is unfair or unequal treatment of an individual (or group) based on certain legally-protected characteristics -- including age, disability, ethnicity, gender, national origin, race, religion

Emmett Louis Till 1941-1955)An African American boy who was murdered in Mississippi in 1955 after allegedly flirting with a white woman, thus becoming an important figure in the Civil Rights movement.

Dred Scott Decision This was the U.S. Supreme Court's ruling on March 6, 1857, that having lived in a free state and territory did not entitle an enslaved person, Dred Scott, to his freedom. In essence, the decision argued that, as someone's property, Scott was not a citizen and could not sue in a federal court.

Egalitarian Asserting, resulting from, or characterized by belief in the equality of all people, especially in political, economic, or social life.

The Emancipation Proclamation An executive order issued by President Abraham Lincoln on January 1, 1863, as the country entered the third year of the Civil War. It declared that all persons held as slaves ... shall be then, thenceforward, and forever free—but it applied only to states designated as being in rebellion, not to the slave-holding border states of Delaware, Kentucky, Maryland, and Missouri or to areas of the Confederacy that had already come under Union control. The careful planning of this document, with Lincoln releasing it at just the right moment in the war, ensured that it had a great positive impact on the Union efforts and redefined the purpose of the war. The 13th Amendment formally abolished slavery.

Executive Order 9981 Executive Order 9981, issued by President Harry S. Truman on July 26, 1948, committed the government to integrating the United States military. The order stated, There shall be equality of treatment and opportunity for all persons in the armed forces without regard to race, color, religion, or national origin. The order was met with some resistance by the military, but by the end of the Korean conflict, nearly all branches were integrated.

Federalize to place under the authority of the federal government

FMLA Short for the Family and Medical Leave Act, which applies to employers who have more than fifty employees on their payroll. The FMLA prohibits employers from discriminating against employees who choose to take time off of work to care for certain medical needs of their own, or to care for their family members, including newborn and adopted children

Freedom Rides Freedom Rides were a series of protests between May and November 1961, when about four hundred volunteers rode buses and trains into the South to challenge racial segregation in public transportation. Supreme Court rulings in 1946 (Morgan v. Commonwealth of Virginia) and 1960 (Boynton v. Virginia) outlawed racial segregation in interstate buses and railways and in associated facilities such as dining counters, waiting rooms, and restrooms. Despite these federal court decisions, many parts of the South continued to enforce local segregation laws.

Ghetto A part of a city in which members of a minority group live because of social or legal pressure

Great Migration The Great Migration was the voluntary emigration of a large number of African Americans from the southern United States to areas in the Northeast, Midwest, and West between 1910 and 1930. Migrants were searching for employment in industrial cities, educational opportunities, and an escape from the discrimination and segregation imposed by Jim Crow laws in the South. The migration was also partially inspired by the South's struggling agricultural system, which left many African Americans poor and jobless. A second migration of African Americans from the South took place between the years 1940 and 1970. These years of emigration altered the demographic structure of the nation and changed the cultural, political, economic, and social lives of African Americans.

Harass To worry and annoy repeatedly

Harlem Renaissance The Harlem Renaissance was a cultural movement in the 1920s and 1930s that took place in New York City's Harlem neighborhood. Home to a large number of middle-class blacks, Harlem was a cultural center for the African American community and was referred to as the capital of black America. First called the New Negro movement, the Harlem Renaissance was a time of change in the black community, when literature and the arts flourished.

Individuals with Disabilities in Education Act (IDEA) A federal law that guarantees the right to a free and appropriate education to disabled students

Hegemony The dominance of one group over another, often supported by legitimating norms and ideas. The term hegemony is today often used as shorthand to describe the relatively dominant position of a particular set of ideas and their associated tendency to become commonsensical and intuitive, thereby inhibiting the dissemination or even the articulation of alternative ideas.

Indict To charge with a crime

Injustice The absence of justice; violation of the rights of another

Integration The act of bringing about equal membership in society

Interposition The action of a state whereby its power is placed between its citizens and the federal government

Intimidation The act of making fearful or deterring by threat

Jim Crow Laws The name Jim Crow comes from a song in a minstrel show that was popular in the nineteenth century. The systematic practice of discriminating against and segregating Black people, especially as practiced in the American South from the end of Reconstruction to the mid-20th century. Some examples of Jim Crow laws are the segregation of public schools, public places, and public transportation, and the segregation of restrooms, restaurants, and drinking fountains for whites and blacks. The U.S. military was also segregated.

Ku Klux Klan A secret terrorist society begun after the Civil War that advocates white supremacy; a hate group

Liberal/Progressive Advocate of civil liberties and social progressivism according to which societal practices need to be changed whenever necessary for the greater good of society

Libertarian A political philosophy and movement that upholds liberty as a core principle. Libertarians seek to maximize political freedom and autonomy, emphasizing individualism

Lynching Execution-style murder of a person, often by hanging. There were lynchings across the South in the 1800s and 1900s, usually by white mobs who killed black men, some of whom were accused of crimes. One lynching that occurred in Jackson killed a black woman who was accused of poisoning a white woman. The white woman's husband was later suspected of the poisoning.

March on Washington for Jobs and Freedom (1963) The March on Washington for Jobs and Freedom was a civil rights demonstration held on Wednesday, August 28, 1963 in Washington, D.C. More than two hundred thousand people gathered peacefully to promote social and economic equality for African Americans.

Middle Passage The middle passage was the middle, or second, leg of the transatlantic trade triangle used to transport goods and slaves between Europe, Africa, and the Americas. In the first leg, ships loaded with goods from Europe traveled to West Africa, where their cargo was traded for imprisoned Africans destined for slavery. Once loaded with the human cargo, the ships sailed to the Caribbean or North or South America. This leg of the trip, referred to as the middle passage, lasted between six and eight weeks. The close quarters and deplorable conditions in which the Africans were held led to suicide attempts, the spread of disease, and death

National Association for the Advancement of Colored People (NAACP) Founded in 1909 by a group of social and political activists in New York, the National Association for the Advancement of Colored People (NAACP) is the nation's oldest, largest, and most widely recognized grassroots-based civil rights organization. Mary White Ovington, Ida B. Wells, W. E. B. Du Bois, Henry Moskowitz, and William English Walling formed the organization in response to the practice of lynching and the 1908 race riot in Springfield, Illinois. They wished to promote equality and eradicate racial discrimination.

Nullification In United States constitutional history, is a legal theory that a state has the right to nullify, or invalidate, any federal law which that state has deemed unconstitutional with respect to the United States Constitution (as opposed to the state's own constitution). The theory of nullification has never been legally upheld by federal courts.

Montgomery Bus Boycott: The Montgomery bus boycott was a 381-day protest of the segregated seating policies on Montgomery, Alabama's public transit system. The boycott began on December 1, 1955, when Rosa Parks, a black seamstress, was arrested for refusing the bus driver's order to give her seat to a white man. The Montgomery bus boycott was instrumental in bringing the nation's attention to civil rights issues and made Martin Luther King Jr. a leading figure in the movement.

Nationalism Ideology based on the idea that the individual's loyalty and devotion to the nation-state surpass other individual or group interests.

Nonviolent civil disobedience the act of protesting laws while not hurting other people or destroying property

Nonviolent direct action doing something to bring examples of injustice to the attention of others

Nonviolent resistance the act of peacefully exerting oneself to counteract something

Open housing A principle in which people may live in whichever neighborhood they can afford regardless of their race

Oppression Unjust or cruel exercise of authority or power

Ordinance Laws set forth by a government authority

Quid Pro Quo: A Latin phrase meaning something for something.

Patriotism The quality of being patriotic; devotion to and vigorous support for one's country.

Picket To walk or stand in from of; to protest

Poll tax A tax or fixed amount per person levied on adults before they can vote

Plessy v. Ferguson The Supreme Court Decision that created the idea of separate but equal and was the basis for segregation and most of the Jim Crow laws.

Prayer vigil A time of keeping watch and praying

Public Works of Art Project During the Great Depression, the Public **Works of Art Project** (PWAP) was the first of the New Deal art programs that put unemployed visual artists to work. Between December 1933 and June 1934, the PWAP funded 3,750 artists who produced 15,600 artworks at a cost of $1,312,000. The enormous success of this program spawned several other New Deal arts initiatives.

Reconstruction Reconstruction is the name of the period immediately following the Civil War, from 1865 to 1877, when the issue of restoring the South was addressed. The passing of the Thirteenth, Fourteenth, and Fifteenth Amendments provided African Americans with new freedoms, but enforcement of the rights granted by these amendments proved difficult in the southern states. Reconstruction changed race relations in America, brought the first public schools to the south, and allowed for the election of several African Americans to political offices on local and state levels.

Redlining The systematic denial by financial institutions and local government of mortgages, insurance, loans, and other financial services based on location rather than on an individual's creditworthiness. A policy mostly directed at residents of minority neighborhoods.

Segregation The act of keeping people of different races apart

Sit-in A method of nonviolent direct action or civil disobedience where people refuse to leave a restaurant or other establishment until their demands are met

Southern Christian Leadership Conference (SCLC) An organization created in 1957 by southern black leaders to work for equality among races

States' Rights It is a term used to describe the ongoing struggle over political power in the United States between the federal government and individual states as broadly outlined in the Tenth Amendment and whether the USA is a single entity or an amalgamation of independent nations. In modern times the term States Rights has also come to symbolize the opposition of some states to federal mandated laws against racial segregation and discrimination. In the 19th Century, States' rights was an argument for maintaining the institution slavery.

Student Nonviolent Coordinating Committee (SNCC) An organization established by students in the late 1950's to coordinate student protests and sponsor voter registration drives

Tyranny Oppressive power

Whistleblower A whistleblower is an employee who reports a violation of the law by his or her employer.

White nationalist One is a type of nationalism or pan-nationalism which espouses the belief that white people are a race and seeks to develop and maintain a white racial and national identity. Many of its proponents identify with and are attached to the concept of a white nation.

Appendices

APPENDIX A

Survey Questions 1: *What is Biblical Justice?*

R1: It is Yahweh's instructions for doing right by others as it is revealed primarily in the Hebrew Scriptures. It is what the Hebrew Scriptures reveal about one of the attributes of Yahweh's character and his dealings with mankind.

R2: Based on the writings of Moses in the Pentateuch, Biblical justice is the application of God's law in society to achieve an equitable, fair, and impartial application of the rule of God's commandments, statues, and ordinances economically, politically, socially, and to administer both civil and criminal justice, according to God's law.

R3: Biblical justice is to do what is right and just.

R4: Application of God's word to a given situation

R5: I believe Biblical Justice as defined in the New Testament and demonstrated in the life of Jesus is to provide equal mercy, grace, and resources to all alike regardless of position, racial background, or gender.

R6: Biblical Justice is a broad spectrum depending upon where one's paradigm begins. For example, in the Old Testament Moses writes: "But if any harm follows, then you shall give life for life, eye for eye, tooth for tooth, hand for hand, foot for foot, burn for burn, wound for wound, stripe for stripe." (Exodus 21:23-25)

However, in the New Testament Jesus gives a very different prescription: "You have heard that it was said, 'An eye for an eye and a tooth for a tooth.' But I tell you not to resist an evil person. But whoever slaps you on your right cheek, turn the other to him also." (Matthew 5:38-39)

The stark contrast between the two is not about trying to find a balance, where one tries to decide when it is okay to poke out the other person's eye or allow themselves to turn the other cheek. Rather, this comes down to an inner point of reference. Is the response retributive or compassionate? Therein is the issue; they are not equal. If one finds himself or herself calling themselves a Christian, then Christ's words usurps Moses (for a series of reasons), but most importantly in following Jesus as Lord. Still, throughout the New Testament it is evident that one's behavior, especially violence, should be stopped, but again what is the intention when we stop it; retributive or compassionate?

Biblical justice then is a resemblance of the Image and Likeness of Christ being expressed through both individual and group. One could rephrase it and say, "What is the Kingdom of Heaven's justice?" Answer: That which is modeled by the life of Jesus Christ.

Survey Question #2: *Are there any circumstances in which the Bible should be accepted as civil law?*

R1: When the Scriptures uphold the dignity and the just treatment of human life for all of its citizens then those passages should be included as civil law. However, the Bible was primarily written for Christ-Followers. Society and its laws are not the Kingdom of God. Christ-Followers are should represent that Kingdom in every sphere of life, whether Biblical truth are incorporated into civil law or not

R2: The Bible should be probably be accepted as civil law only in a Theocratic society. I can't think of such a society. Since under the New Covenant, the laws of God are written in the Believer's heart (Jer. 31:33), there would be no need to have the Bible to be accepted as civil law.

R3: Yes certain of the commandments such as thou shalt no steal or kill or bear false witness.

R4: Probably several instances including abortion, fornication., etc.

R5: I think that the principles of the Bible should, but in these times it should be written into the civil law with civil language and a justification for it. The First Amendment has been good for religious groups in the US and I would be concerned how the Bible taken straight might be used by people who do not understand it.

R6: This can be a real "cart before the horse" question. If the Bible (as most Christians would say) is a spiritual book, then without that component, it is just another set of laws subject to the tribe who uses it. Remember, the Ku Klux Klan uses the Bible as its governing volume, and so they would agree the Bible should be accepted as civil law. The issue isn't the Bible, but the hearts and minds that implement it. On the other hand, if the hearts are Christ-Centered, as sighted in earlier answers, the Bible itself isn't necessary to be accepted as civil law; it's done by nature.

Survey Question #3: *What is racism and what is the source of it?*

R1: White Supremacy is the source and racism is its behavior.

R2: Historically, the source "race' is a social construct invented by whites to seize and retain economic and social power by the marginalization and oppression of people of color based on this socially constructed racial hierarchy that privileges white people and devalues people of color.

R3: Race

R4: Prejudice or discrimination directed toward a person or ethnic group. Disobedience to the word of God

R5: Racism is the view of a dominant race that other minority races are inferior or less deserving of justice. The sources are selfishness, fear, pride, and ignorance.

R6: In sociology, racism is the abusive and aggressive behavior towards another race based on the belief that there are intrinsic differences between the races, with the focus that one's own race as superior to another.

The source is twofold. Most would say racism is taught, which is highly true. Most definitely a tribal environment, from the nuclear family to the community can instill racist values and paradigms to those born within it, or those who join it. However, I would like to add an additional aspect: The fallen human nature, or one could say, the egoistic nature. This is also known as Mimetic Impulse. The ego is comparative. For example, we find our identities through comparing what gives us pleasure in comparison to what doesn't, and most importantly where we find acceptance and affirmation. Thus, you can have two three-year-old children of different races playing in a sandbox together and all is well. Then comes the impulse for one to take the other's plastic shovel because he or she likes the color or size better than theirs. The response is the one starts crying and hits the other with their pail and a lot of crying and hitting ensues.

This could end with the two forgiving and making up because they may actually like or even love each other (which would be a rather highly developed sense of inner self for a typical three-year-old). Yet, the ego was at work when the one took the shovel and the other hit with the pail. The other more common way this could end is with more anger, name calling, finger pointing, and judgments about the other. Those almost thoughtless judgments can develop into stronger self-centered views, "Their whole family is like that." "I feel uncomfortable around people who look like them, because of what they did." And of course, the basest of such impulses, "Those people are all like that." The racism that is taught is a developed social view that originated in a base egoistic impulse from fear, anger and self-centeredness.

Survey Question #4: *Is abortion murder?*

R1: There are ethical considerations and health considerations to this answer. If the view that human life begins at the fetus, then the extermination of that life by the will of the pregnant woman could be considered murder by Christians. However, if the view that human life begins after birth abortion is the extermination of the fetus and could not be murder, if view from a purely human standpoint. There are medical complications that could prevent a successful birth to both the mother and child. My position is that abortion should only be considered if it poses the threat to the human life of the pregnant woman or wife.

R2: Yes, in the strictest moral sense; however, it is not murder Biblically or civilly. Even if abortion were murder in some way; murder is a sin, and God forgives sin.

R3: I think it would be closer to man slaughter.

R4: Of course.

R5: Abortion is killing, but if we really believed it was actual murder we would do more than march twice a year.

R6: Context is everything; cannot give a one-dimensional answer. Blanket answers on such topics tend to gender inequitable results.

Survey Question #5: *What Biblical justice should be meted out for those who get abortions or perform abortions?*

R1: God honors human choice/will. There is no Scripture that I know of where Yahweh punished his followers who engaged in an act of abortion. Fundamental theologians have tried to equate abortion to child sacrifice to give it a grossly evil connotation. This is a stretch and eisegesis at worse.

R2: None. If abortion is a sin, for those who get abortions or perform abortions, their sin should be forgiven. God is a God of mercy and forgiveness. Man should never impose his sense of imperfect morality into Biblical justice.

R3: They should receive the similar penalty one would receive for man slaughter.

R4: Tried as murders under civil laws.

R5: Abortion has existed throughout history. Yet the Bible is strangely silent on this issue. I feel that the church's role is to persuade, work to make abortion rare or non existent, deal with the issues of poverty and violence that leave young mothers with horrible choices so that they can have hope for better outcomes.

R6: Again, context is everything and each situation looked at individually. As the former president of a crisis pregnancy center for over a decade, the sanctity of human life is especially important. However, that sanctity is not limited to the unborn; all aspects of the situation must be taken into account. This includes our willingness to assist the mother, if necessary, with finances, supplies, emotional and spiritual support, our time and presence.

Survey Question #4: *What can Christians do to become more unified and to positively impact communities?*

R1: Continue down the path of education. Seek to find projects that advance the common good for all people. Respect all human life and be the first to be an example of it.

R2: If Christians practiced and kept the commandments of Jesus to love neighbors and one another, and ascribed priority and high value to this God kind of love and commit to unswerving genuine unity—not just "lip service", this love and unity—transcending race, nativism, and church denomination—will positively impact communities (John 13:35; 15:17).

R3: Reject the sin of racism in all its forms and inform as many people as possible about this diabolical doctrine that still divides the nation and the church.

R4: How about following the word of God for starters.

R5: I don't know.

R6: Something I have been saying at our church and in places I have been asked to speak as I travel is: "We need to be a Christ-centered people, using the Bible as a tool; not a Bible centered people hoping and assuming Christ will be a result." These two concepts are drastically different.

Another key which amplifies the point would be to return to the first several hundred years of theology known as Christus Victor (the victorious Christ) and undo the western development of the medieval theology of "Satisfaction Theory" by Anselme du Bec, Catholic Archbishop of Canterbury, which was adapted by the Church in the end of the first millennia. This was the product of the earlier Constantinian era and its adaptation and renunciation of the doctrine of "ultimate reconciliation" in 533 AD. Then also to seriously rethink and undo its fully developed version instituted by John Calvin, known as the doctrine of Penal Substitution or Vicarious Atonement Theory. In the name of unifying the Church, all the above actually fragmented the Church and empowered the justification of anti-Semitism, racism, slavery, and supremacy. While the belief in Eastern religious philosophies is, if one is a slave, or of a particular race, or of a social status in a caste system, we should not change that because it can affect their Karma; the Church took that thinking to another level. Now it was not just about Karma, it was about judgment and even eternal damnation. The Church will consistently struggle with being unified and making a community impact (I say this as the former president of our city's ministerial association for 17 years), by seeing "the other (Christian)" as either compromising God's Word, or in some form of sin because of one's difference, thus our unity becomes very superficial. For example, as one "black" minister said to me, "I can't support Black Lives Matter, because it was started by lesbians." So, what does one think of those ministers who support Black Lives Matter? How do we stand together against racism with such technicalities? In my view, this can be seen as a form of the injustice, both Biblical and civil, within our own ranks that was discussed throughout this research project.

In conclusion, like the Holy Roman Empire, the American Church (regardless of denomination) must, and in my current view is going through, a reformation within itself as it steps into the arena of the community. We cannot wait for the first to happen then step into the community; they must happen simultaneously.

APPENDIX B

Definitions of the Word Justice as Used in the Bible

(**Note:** Following is an overview of Bible words, not a exegesis of the text. *Exegesis* means using the words of the Scripture text, through the lens of their original context, to determine their intent.)

Let's begin with reading Psalms 89:14 from the King James Version and the New International Version.

KJV: ***Justice*** *and **judgment** are the habitation of thy throne: mercy and truth shall go before thy face.*

NIV: ***Righteousness*** *and **justice** are the foundation of your throne; love and faithfulness go before you.*

Notice the word differences between the translations:

KJV *Justice* = NIV *Righteousness*

KJV *Judgment* = NIV *Justice*

In the King James Version, the word *justice* is usually the Hebrew word מִשְׁפָּט (the male noun "mishpat," Strong's H4941).

Strong's H4941 is defined: "The act of deciding a case, seat of judgment, procedure, litigation (before judges), case, cause (presented for judgment), sentence, decision (of judgment), execution (of judgment).

In newer translations, such as the New International Version, *justice* is usually the word צְדָקָה (the female noun "tsedaqah," Strong's H6666)

Strong's H6666 defined: "Righteousness (in government), of a judge, ruler, king. Righteousness (as of God's attribute). Rightness, righteousness (as ethically right), righteous acts.

Returning to the previous Scriptures, we will add the Strong's numbers: H4941 as *justice/judgment:* and H6666 as *justice/righteousness*

He has shown you, O man, what is good; And what does the Lord require of you but to do justly (H4941), to love mercy, and to walk humbly with your God? (Micah 6:8)

Thus says the Lord: "Execute judgment (H4941) and righteousness (H6666), and deliver the plundered out of the hand of the oppressor. Do no wrong and do no violence to the stranger, the fatherless, or the widow, nor shed innocent blood in this place." (Jeremiah 22:3)

Learn to do good; Seek justice (H4941), Rebuke the oppressor; Defend the fatherless, Plead for the widow. (Isaiah 1:17)

Blessed are those who keep justice (H4941), And he who does righteousness at all times! (Psalm 106:3)

It is a joy for the just to do justice (H4941), But destruction will come to the workers of iniquity. (Proverbs 21:15)

Notes

In Order of Appearance in the Book

Jones, Robert P., *White Too Long: The Legacy of White Supremacy in American Christianity*. Publisher: Simon & Schuster. 2020

Mason, Eric. *Woke Church*. Moody Publishers. 2018

Marshall, Chris. *Little Book of Biblical Justice: A Fresh Approach To The Bible's Teachings On Justice*. Good Books, 2005

Gobry, P. *What the Bible really says about government*. 2020, from https://theweek.com/articles/779283/what-bible-really-says-about-government.

Gardner, S. E.. *Leading the practice of social justice through Evangelical congregations: A multi-case study*. Dissertation Abstracts International Section A: Humanities and Social Sciences. ProQuest Information & Learning. 2016

What does social justice really mean? World Vision. 2020. https://www.worldvision.org/blog/social-justice-really-mean

Magee, Malcolm. *The Dark Side of Religion in America*. 2019. https://medium.com/@malcolmmagee/the-dark-side-of-religion-in-america-194b5e2fce9f

Taylor, D. B. *Who Were the Freedom Riders?* 2020. https://www.ytimes.com/#publisher. https://www.nytimes.com/2020/07/18/us/politics/freedom-riders-john-lewis-work.html

Chicago is far from the U.S. 'murder capital.' 2018. Pew Research Center. https://www.pewresearch.org/fact-tank/2018/11/13/despite-recent-violence-chicago-far-from-u-s-murder-capital/

Rutherford B. Hayes. *The White House.* 2020 https://www.whitehouse.gov/about-the-white-house/presidents/rutherford-b-hayes/

Reconstruction. History Channel https://www.history.com/topics/american-civil-war/reconstruction

The Black Codes and Jim Crow Laws. National Geographic Society. 2020 https://www.nationalgeographic.org/encyclopedia/black-codes-and-jim-crow-laws/

King, M. L. *Letter From Birmingham Jail.* The Atlantic. 1965. https://www.theatlantic.com/magazine/archive/2018/02/letter-from-a-birmingham-jail/552461/

MacFarquhar, N. *Many Claim Extremists Are Sparking Protest Violence. But Which Extremists?* New York Times. 2020 https://www.nytimes.com/2020/05/31/us/george-floyd-protests-white-supremacists-antifa.html

Changing Company *Culture Requires a Movement, Not a Mandate.* Harvard Business Review. 2017 https://hbr.org/2017/06/changing-company-culture-requires-a-movement-not-a-mandate

Waldman, K. *A Sociologist Examines the "White Fragility" That Prevents White Americans from Confronting Racism.* The New Yorker. 2018 https://www.newyorker.com/books/page-turner/a-sociologist-examines-the-white-fragility-that-prevents-white-americans-from-confronting-racism

Roach, D. *Most US Pastors Speak Out in Response to George Floyd's Death.* Christianity Today. 2020 https://www.christianitytoday.com/news/2020/june/pastors-george-floyd-racism-church-barna-research.html

Post-traumatic stress disorder (PTSD) - Symptoms and causes. Mayo Clinic. 2018 https://www.mayoclinic.org/diseases-conditions/post-traumatic-stress-disorder/symptoms-causes/syc-20355967

World Among Federal Violent Offenders. United States Sentencing Commission. 2019 https://www.ussc.gov/sites/default/files/pdf/research-and-publications/research-publications/2019/20190124RecidivismViolence.pdf

Woodson, Carter G. *The Mis-Education of the Negro* 1933 (Public Domain). Kindle Edition.

Core 40 General Information | IDOE. Indiana Department of Education. 2011 https://www.doe.in.gov/school-improvement/student-assistance/core-40-general-information

Wesley, C. *The Mis-Education of the Negro - Introduction by Charles H. Wesley*. History Is A Weapon. 1969 https://www.historyisaweapon.com/defcon1/misedne.html

Sullivan, Kenneth. *Abeka and Inclusion: An Analysis of the Degree to Which the Abeka Curriculum Includes the Contributions of People of African Descent*. Trinity College of the Bible and Theological Seminary. 2005 http://visioncomsolutionscom.siteprotect.net/AbekaCurriculumSullivanDissertation.pdf

Greczyn, A. *Christianity's Role in American Racism: An Uncomfortable Look at the Present and the Past.* 2020

America's racial reckoning must happen, leaders say at MSNBC town hall. NBC News. 2018 https://www.nbcnews.com/news/nbcblk/msnbc-s-everyday-racism-america-racial-reckoning-must-happen-leaders-n878336

Moral Majority | Definition, History, Mission, & Facts. Encyclopedia Britannica. Retrieved 2020 https://www.britannica.com/topic/Moral-Majority

Holland, J. *Abolishing Abortion: The History of the Pro-Life Movement in America* | The American Historian. The American Historian. 2016 https://www.oah.org/tah/issues/2016/november/abolishing-abortion-the-history-of-the-pro-life-movement-in-america/

Cha, A. *U.S. abortion rate fell 25 percent from 2008 to 2014; one in four women have an abortion.* Washington Post. 2017. https://tinyurl.com/y63caphv

Recidivism Among Federal Violent Offenders. United States Sentencing Commission. 2019 https://www.ussc.gov/sites/default/files/pdf/

About The Author

Bryan Hudson has a passion to serve God's purpose in ministry, community, missions to Africa, and digital media. As a senior pastor with more than 38 years experience, empowering people through Bible teaching and practical wisdom is his mission. As an author of 10 books and host of the Firm Foundation Podcast and Blog with over 1000 articles, Bryan is a thinker and commentator on the key issues of our time. Bryan has earned degrees in Bachelor of Theology, Bachelor of Science in Media Arts & Science, Master of Science in Instructional Design, and Doctor of Ministry.

He has been recognized for contributions to the State of Indiana and youth mentoring. For 20 years Bryan conducted multimedia empowerment programs for youth to equip the next generation of digital media producers. For 42 years, Bryan has been married to Patricia Ann Hudson (B.A., M.S.), an inner-city public school educator. They have raised four children, have two grandchildren, and reside in Indianapolis, Indiana.

CONNECT WITH BRYAN HUDSON

Email: info@biblicaljusticebook.com

Blog: BryanHudson.com

Facebook: /BryanHudson

Twitter: @BryanHudson

Book: BiblicalJusticeBook.com

Other Books: VisionBooksMedia.com